HABITAT Arctic foxes live on the coast and islands of the Arctic Ocean. They live in burrows dug in the side of hills or cliffs.

CHARACTERISTICS The arctic fox uses its bushy tail to stay warm.

SELF-PROTECTION A small nose helps the arctic fox live in cold climates.

CAMOUFLAGE In the summer, the fur is short. It is brown, gray, or blue.

Science

Arctic Fox

Harcourt
SCHOOL PUBLISHERS

Orlando   Austin   New York   San Diego   Toronto   London

Visit *The Learning Site!*
www.harcourtschool.com

Printed in the United States of America

ISBN 0-15-348828-X

2 3 4 5 6 7 8 9 10   048   13 12 11 10 09 08 07

Arctic Fox

v

UNIT B
PHYSICAL SCIENCE

160

EARTH AND SPACE SCIENCE

Science Spin
Weekly Reader

Technology
Is the Weather Getting Worse?, 306

People/Careers
Watching the Weather, 308

ARIZONA EXCURSIONS

Your Guide to Science in Arizona

Ready, Set, Science!

Vocabulary
senses
inquiry skills
science tools

I wonder...

Can kids be scientists?

What do YOU wonder?

1

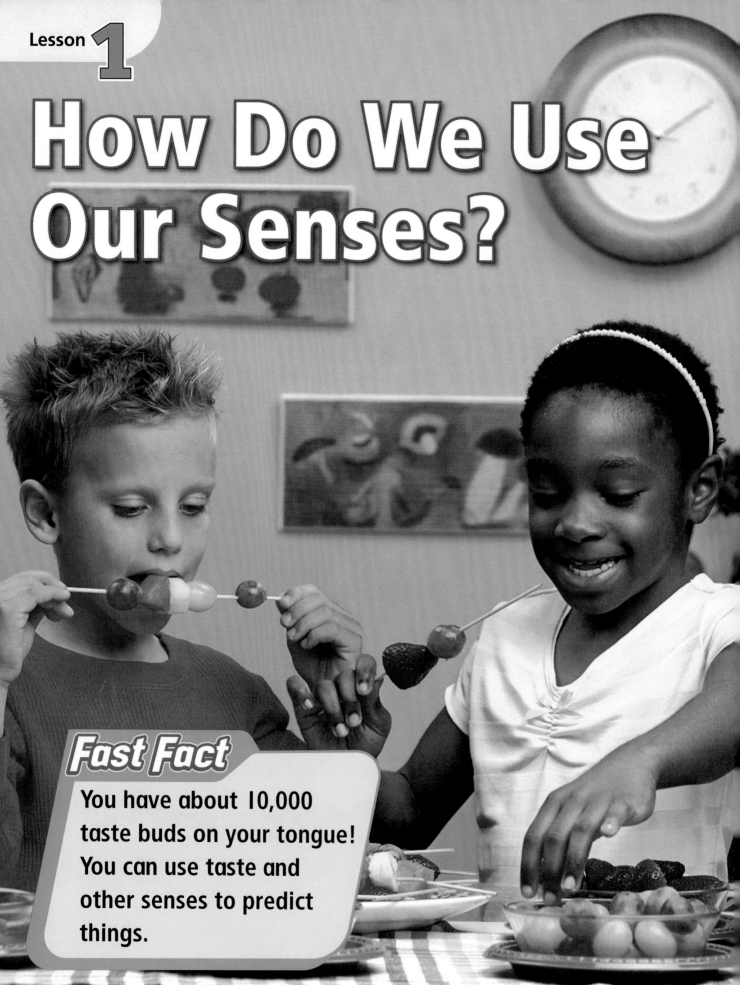

How Do We Use Our Senses?

Fast Fact

You have about 10,000 taste buds on your tongue! You can use taste and other senses to predict things.

How Your Senses Work

You need

• oranges

• bananas

• apples

Step 1

Close your eyes. Your partner will give you a piece of fruit.

Step 2

Smell the fruit. Then taste it. **Predict** which kind of fruit you will see when you open your eyes. Was your **prediction** correct?

Step 3

Trade places with your partner. Repeat.

Inquiry Skill

When you predict, you tell what you think will happen.

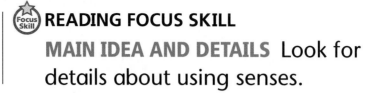

Reading in Science

VOCABULARY
senses

READING FOCUS SKILL

MAIN IDEA AND DETAILS Look for details about using senses.

Your Senses

People have five senses. The five **senses** are sight, hearing, smell, taste, and touch. You use different body parts for different senses.

MAIN IDEA AND DETAILS
What are the five senses?

touch
hear
see
smell
taste

4

Senses Help You

Your senses help you observe and learn about many things.

 MAIN IDEA AND DETAILS
How can your senses help you learn?

What Do You Hear?

Close your eyes, and listen closely to the sounds around you. Predict what sounds you hear. Open your eyes. Were your predictions correct?

Using Senses Safely

Keep your body safe. Use safety equipment when you need to. Follow these safety rules.

MAIN IDEA AND DETAILS
How can you keep safe?

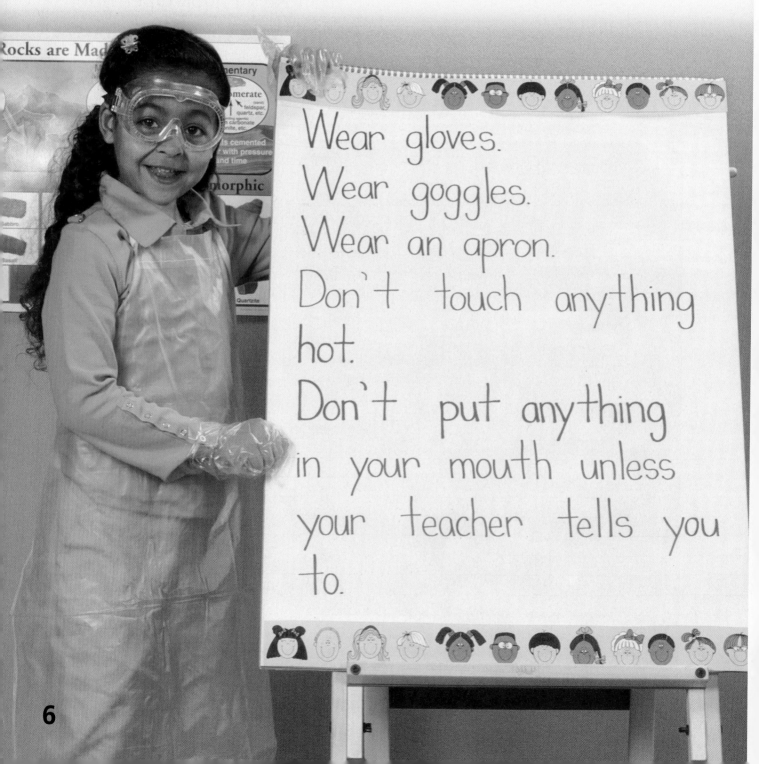

Wear gloves.
Wear goggles.
Wear an apron.
Don't touch anything hot.
Don't put anything in your mouth unless your teacher tells you to.

1. MAIN IDEA AND DETAILS Copy and complete this chart.

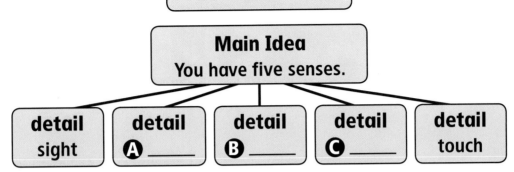

The Five Senses

Main Idea
You have five senses.

detail	detail	detail	detail	detail
sight	Ⓐ _____	Ⓑ _____	Ⓒ _____	touch

2. SUMMARIZE Use the chart to tell about the lesson.

3. VOCABULARY Use the word **senses** to tell about the picture.

Test Prep

4. Which sense do you use when you feel something?
   A. hearing
   B. smell
   C. taste
   D. touch

Writing

Label Senses
Draw a picture of yourself. What body parts do you use to taste, see, smell, touch, and hear? Label the body parts with the correct sense.

 For more links and activities, go to www.hspscience.com

7

How Do We Use Inquiry Skills?

Fast Fact

Pineapples grow on the ground. They have hard, rough peelings. You can draw conclusions about why fruits have peelings.

Fruit Protection

You need

• fruits

• hand lens

Step 1

Observe some fruits with a hand lens. Look at their peelings.

Step 2

Observe the cut fruits with the hand lens. What is inside the fruit?

Step 3

Draw conclusions about why fruits have peelings.

Inquiry Skill

You **draw conclusions** when you use information to figure out why something is the way it is.

VOCABULARY
inquiry skills

 READING FOCUS SKILL

MAIN IDEA AND DETAILS Look for details about the inquiry skills scientists use.

Investigating

Scientists follow steps to test things they want to learn about.

1. Observe, and ask a question.

Ask questions. What do you want to know? You can work alone, with a partner, or in a small group.

Is a balloon filled with air heavier than a balloon without air?

2. Form a hypothesis.

Explore your questions. What do you think will happen?

3. Plan a fair test.

It is important to be fair. This will help you get correct answers to your questions.

I'll tie these at the same spot on each end.

4. Do the test.

Try your test. Repeat your test in different places. You should get the same answers.

5. Draw conclusions. Communicate what you learn.

What did you find out? Compare your answers with those of classmates. Share your answers by talking, drawing, or writing.

MAIN IDEA AND DETAILS What steps do scientists follow to test things?

Using Inquiry Skills

Scientists use inquiry skills when they do tests. **Inquiry skills** help people find out information.

communicate

classify

make a model

hypothesize

The red car will roll farther because it is heavier.

draw conclusions

compare

sequence

measure

14

observe

predict

Life Cycle of a Bean Plant

Seed Sprouting

Seed

Roots

15

plan an investigation

infer

Insta-Lab

How Far Will It Roll?

Get a ball. Predict how far it will go if you roll it across the floor. Mark that spot with tape. Roll the ball. Was your prediction right?

★ **MAIN IDEA AND DETAILS**
Focus Skill
What skills do scientists use when they do tests?

16

1. MAIN IDEA AND DETAILS Copy and complete this chart.

Main Idea
Inquiry skills help people find out information.

detail	detail	detail

measure	**A** _____	**B** _____

2. SUMMARIZE Use the chart to tell about the lesson.

3. VOCABULARY Use the words **inquiry skills** to tell about this picture.

Test Prep

4. What do you do when you compare?

   A. make a guess

   B. observe how things are alike and different

   C. make a plan to do something

   D. show how something works

Links

Math

Grouping Blocks

Get some blocks that are different sizes and colors. Think of ways to classify the blocks. Then classify the blocks in two different ways. Draw a picture of the ways you classified the blocks.

 For more links and activities, go to www.hspscience.com

17

How Do We Use Science Tools?

Fast Fact

A blender is a tool that can help make many things—even medicines! You can use tools to compare things.

Compare Fruit

You need

- strawberry   • pear   • balance

Step 1

Put one piece of fruit on each side of a balance.

Step 2

Compare the masses of the fruits. Record what you see.

Step 3

Which fruit has less mass? Which has more mass?

Inquiry Skill

You **compare** when you observe ways things are alike and different.

19

Reading in Science

VOCABULARY
science tools

 READING FOCUS SKILL

MAIN IDEA AND DETAILS Look for details about science tools.

Using Science Tools

Scientists use tools to find out about things. You can use tools to find out about things, too. **Science tools** help people find information they need.

Some things have parts that are too small to see. You can use a hand lens or a magnifying box to help you see them.

magnifying box and hand lens

forceps

You can use forceps to help you separate things.

20

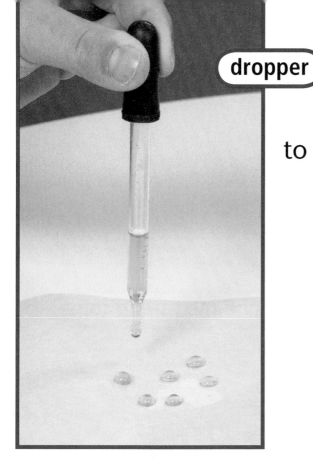

dropper

You can use a dropper
to place drops of liquid.

You can use a measuring
cup to measure liquid.

measuring cup

thermometer

You can use a
thermometer to
measure how hot or
cold something is.

You can use a ruler to measure how long or tall an object is. You can use a measuring tape to measure around an object.

ruler and measuring tape

balance

You can use a balance to measure the mass of an object.

Measure It!
Use a tape measure to measure around your arm. Then measure around your leg. Compare the numbers. Which one is greater?

⭐ MAIN IDEA AND DETAILS
How can you use science tools to find out information?

22

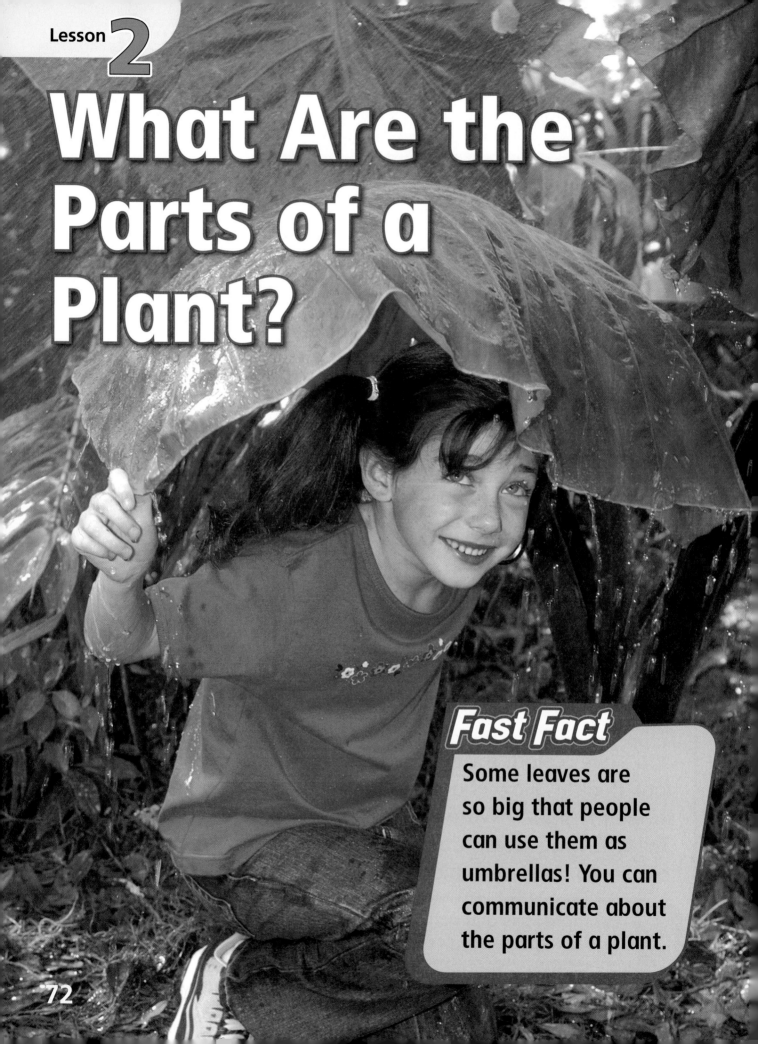

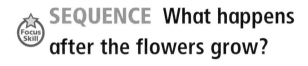

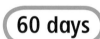

adult tree

small tree

85

adult butterfly

butterfly comes out

pupa

Insta-Lab

Be a Butterfly

Act out a butterfly's life cycle. What happens first, next, and last? How can you move your body to show what happens?

55

Animals and Their Young

Dogs are mammals. The puppies look like their parents, but they are not just like them. They are not just like each other. Each puppy is a little different.

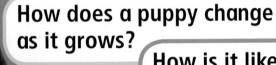

How does a puppy change as it grows?

How is it like its parents?

just-born puppies

adult dog

about 2 months old

For more links and activities, go to www.hspscience.com

56

1. SEQUENCE Copy and complete this chart.

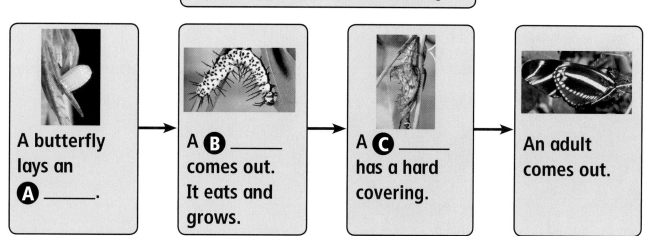

Life Cycle of a Butterfly

A butterfly lays an **A** _____.

→ A **B** _____ comes out. It eats and grows.

→ A **C** _____ has a hard covering.

→ An adult comes out.

2. SUMMARIZE Write sentences that tell what this lesson is about.

3. VOCABULARY Use the word **tadpole** to talk about this picture.

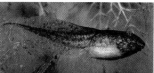

Test Prep

4. Which animal is a larva and a pupa for parts of its life cycle?
   A. a butterfly
   B. a cat
   C. a dog
   D. a frog

Links

Math

Compare Animal Young
This chart shows the number of young some animals may have at one time. Use the data to make a bar graph.

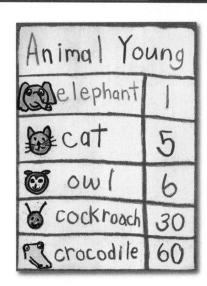

Animal Young

elephant	1
cat	5
owl	6
cockroach	30
crocodile	60

 For more links and activities, go to **www.hspscience.com**

Traveling Turtles:
A Trip Across the Atlantic

In late spring, huge sea turtles crawl onto a beach in Florida. Each turtle digs a nest in the sand. The mother turtle then lays about 100 eggs. Two months later, tiny turtles hatch.

The young turtles crawl out of their holes and into the ocean.

A Long Trip

The tiny turtles set out on a long trip. They swim across the Atlantic Ocean and back again. The trip takes between five and ten years. The trip is thousands of miles long.

Scientists wanted to know how the turtles made their way across the ocean. To find out, scientists put "bathing suits" on some young sea turtles. The bathing suits were tied to machines. The special machines can follow how the turtles swim.

THINK ABOUT IT

How long will it take for a young turtle to swim across the Atlantic Ocean?

Find out more! Log on to **www.hspscience.com**

Feeding Time

Chloe Ruiz went to the petting zoo with her family. Chloe saw pigs, horses, and cows.

The people at the zoo asked Chloe if she wanted to help feed a young cow. A young cow is called a calf.

Chloe fed the calf milk. She used a bottle to feed the calf. She knows the calf needs to drink lots of milk to help it grow.

60

Which Foods Birds Eat

What to Do

1. Put bread crumbs in one pie plate. Put fruit in the other.

2. Put both plates on a table outside.

3. Observe the birds that eat from each plate. Draw pictures to record your observations.

Materials
- 2 foil pie plates
- bread crumbs
- chopped apples and grapes

Draw Conclusions

Do different birds eat different foods? How do you know?

Animals and Their Young

Mammals and most birds care for their young. Choose one. Find out how it helps its young. Make models to show how the animal cares for its young.

Review and Test Preparation

Vocabulary Review

Tell which picture goes best with each word.

1. mammal p. 44   **3. fish** p. 47

2. bird p. 45   **4. insect** p. 48

A.    **B.**    **C.**    **D.**

Check Understanding

5. Show the **sequence**. Write **first**, **next**, **then**, and **last**.

A.    **B.**    **C.**    **D.**

6. Which is **true** about frogs?

    A. They are fish.

    B. They have scaly, dry skin.

    C. The young are called tadpoles.

    D. Adults breathe with gills.

Critical Thinking

7. Compare the pigs. Which one is living? Which is not? Tell how you know.

8. Think about a pet you want. Draw a picture of the pet. List each thing it needs. Tell how you would help it meet its needs.

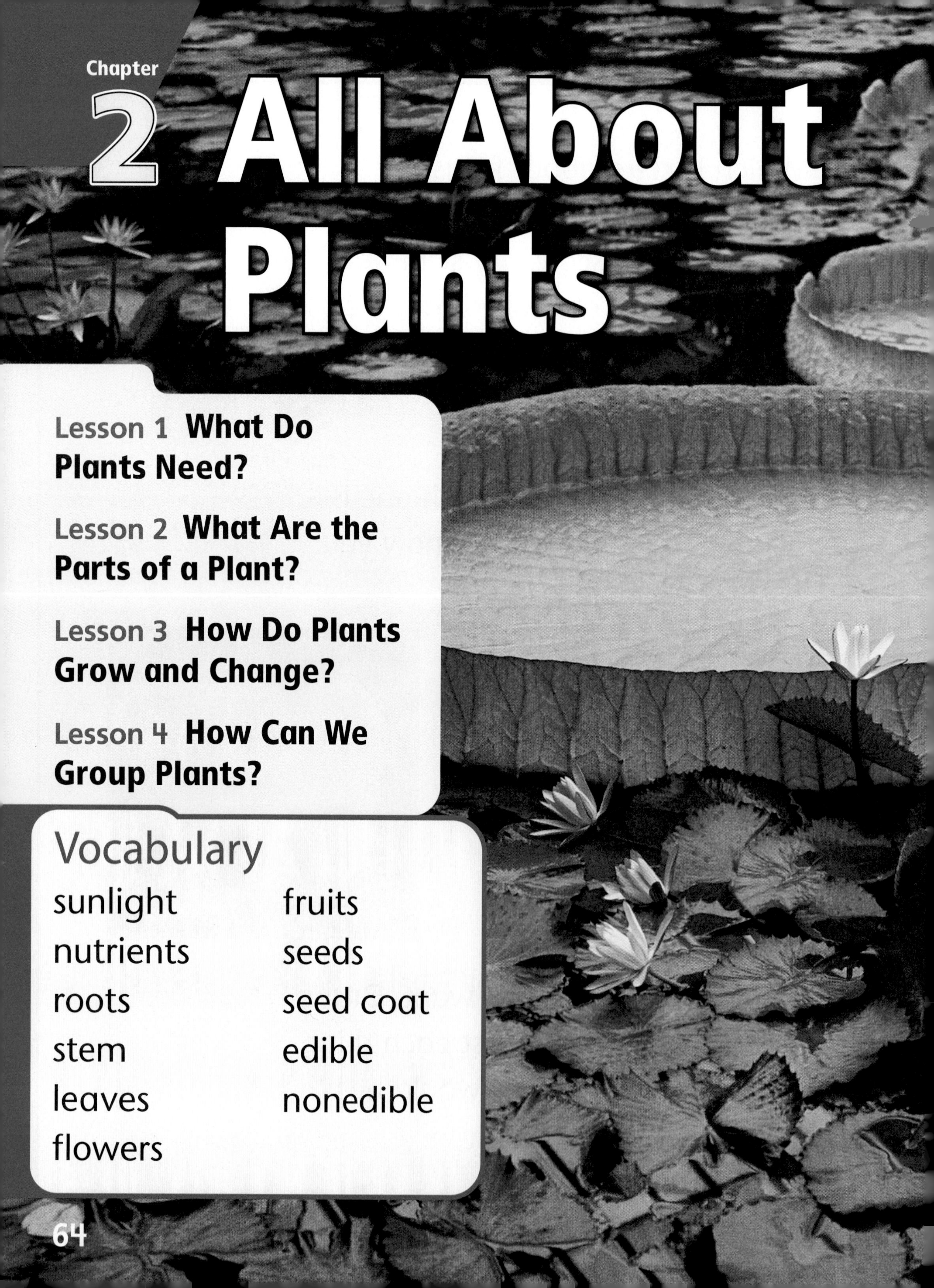

Chapter 2

All About Plants

Vocabulary

sunlight
nutrients
roots
stem
leaves
flowers
fruits
seeds
seed coat
edible
nonedible

I wonder...

Why do plants need water?

What do **YOU** wonder?

What Do Plants Need?

Fast Fact

Orchids have roots that take water from the air. Predict what might happen if there were not enough water in the air.

Predict What Plants Need

You need

- index cards
- 2 small plants
- spray bottle

Step 1

Label the plants. Put both plants in a sunny place.

Step 2

Water only one plant each day. **Predict** what will happen to each plant.

Step 3

After four days, check the plants. Did you **predict** correctly?

Inquiry Skill

To **predict**, use what you know to make a good guess about what will happen.

VOCABULARY
sunlight
nutrients

 READING FOCUS SKILL

CAUSE AND EFFECT Look for all the things that cause plants to grow.

Light, Air, and Water

A plant needs light, air, and water to make its own food. The food helps the plant grow and stay healthy. A plant also needs water to move the food to all its parts.

water

Plants take in **sunlight**, or light from the sun. They take in water mostly from the soil.

CAUSE AND EFFECT

What would happen to a plant that did not have light, air, or water?

Insta-Lab

Make a Model Plant

Use paper, clay, craft sticks, and other art materials to make a model plant. Then tell about what a real plant needs to live.

69

Soil

Plants take in nutrients from the soil.
Nutrients are minerals that plants use
to make their food.

⭐ Focus Skill **CAUSE AND EFFECT** Why does a plant need nutrients?

soil

1. CAUSE AND EFFECT Copy and complete this chart.

Needs of Plants

cause

A plant gets light, **Ⓐ** _____, **Ⓑ** _____, and nutrients.

effect

The plant grows and stays **Ⓒ** _____.

2. DRAW CONCLUSIONS
What would happen if a plant did not get all the things it needed? Tell why.

3. VOCABULARY Use the words **sunlight** and **nutrients** to tell about this picture.

Test Prep
4. Why is soil important to plants?

Links

Writing

Write a Plan
You have a plant that does not look healthy. How could you make it healthy again? Write a plan. Tell what you would do. Draw a picture to show your plan.

 For more links and activities, go to www.hspscience.com

I would give it water each day.

71

What Are the Parts of a Plant?

Fast Fact

Some leaves are so big that people can use them as umbrellas! You can communicate about the parts of a plant.

Parts of a Plant

You need

- crayons

- hand lens

- plant

Step 1

Observe the parts of the plant. Use a hand lens.

Step 2

Draw what you see. Write about your picture.

Step 3

Share your work with a partner. **Communicate** what you observed.

Inquiry Skill

You can use drawing, writing, and talking to **communicate** what you observe.

73

VOCABULARY

roots   flowers
stem   fruits
leaves   seeds

 READING FOCUS SKILL

MAIN IDEA AND DETAILS Look for the parts of a plant and details about what the parts do.

Parts of a Plant

Plants have different parts. The parts help the plant live and grow. Most kinds of plants have roots, a stem, leaves, and flowers.

 MAIN IDEA AND DETAILS
What are some parts of a plant?

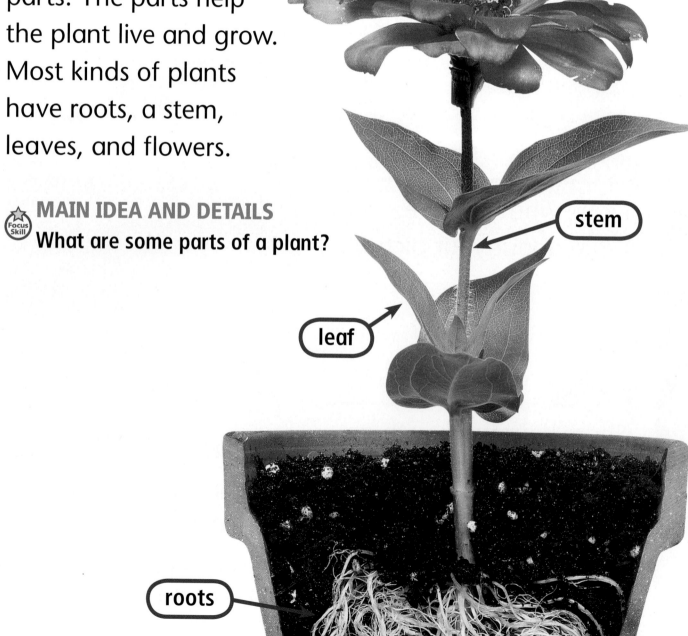

flower

stem

leaf

roots

74

Roots

The **roots** hold the plant in the soil. They also take in the water and nutrients the plant needs.

 MAIN IDEA AND DETAILS
What are two ways roots help a plant?

How Roots Help Plants
Push a craft stick deep into clay. Push another craft stick into clay just a little. Tap the side of each stick. What happens? How is the first stick like a plant with roots? How do roots hold a plant in place?

Where are the roots on these plants?

75

Stems

The **stem** holds up the plant. It carries water and nutrients through the plant.

Stems may be green or woody. The trunks of trees are woody stems.

⭐ **MAIN IDEA AND DETAILS**
Focus Skill
What are two ways the stem helps a plant?

Where are the stems on these plants?

Leaves

Leaves take in light and air. They need these things to make food for the plant. Different kinds of plants have leaves that look different. Leaves have different shapes and patterns.

 **MAIN IDEA AND DETAILS**
What do leaves do?

> **What shapes and patterns do these leaves have?**

Flowers, Fruits, and Seeds

Many plants have flowers. The **flowers** make fruits. The **fruits** hold seeds.

New plants may grow from the **seeds**. The new plants look like the plants that made the seeds.

Focus Skill
MAIN IDEA AND DETAILS

What do flowers do?

flower

seeds

fruit

1. MAIN IDEA AND DETAILS Copy and complete this chart.

Main Idea and Details

The parts of a plant help it live and grow.

The roots take in **A** _____ and **B** _____ from the soil.	The **C** _____ holds up the plant.	The leaves make **D** _____ for the plant.	The flowers make **E** _____. The fruits hold **F** _____.

2. SUMMARIZE Use the vocabulary words to write a lesson summary.

3. VOCABULARY Use the words **stem**, **leaves**, and **flower** to tell about this picture.

Test Prep

4. Which part of the plant makes food?
   A. roots
   B. leaves
   C. flowers
   D. fruits

Links

Math

Measuring Leaves
Put some leaves under a sheet of paper. Rub over the leaves with unwrapped crayons. Measure the rubbings with small blocks. How many blocks long is each leaf?

 For more links and activities, go to www.hspscience.com

Lesson **3**

How Do Plants Grow and Change?

Fast Fact

Coconuts come from coconut palms. They are the world's biggest seeds. You can sequence the parts of a plant's life.

80

From Seed to Plant

You need

- seeds

- 2 clear cups

- colored cup

- soil

Step 1

Fill one clear cup with soil. Plant two seeds near the side. Water the seeds.

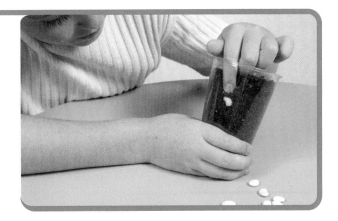

Step 2

Put the clear cup into the colored cup. Take it out each day, draw the seeds, and put it back.

Step 3

After three days, **sequence** your pictures to show what happened to the seeds.

Inquiry Skill

When you **sequence** things, you say what happened first, next, then, and last.

81

READING FOCUS SKILL

SEQUENCE Look for what happens first, next, then, and last as a seed grows into a plant.

How Plants Grow

Most plants grow from seeds. Some seeds have a seed coat. A **seed coat** is a covering that protects the seed. Inside the seed is a tiny plant. If the seed gets water, air, and warmth, the plant in it may start to grow.

seed

seed coat

15 days

First, the roots grow down into the soil. Next, a stem grows up. Then, leaves and flowers grow. Last, the flowers make fruits that hold seeds. The seeds may grow into new plants.

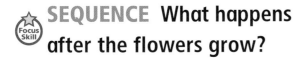 **SEQUENCE** What happens after the flowers grow?

60 days

45 days

Insta-Lab

What's Inside?
Peel the seed coat off a bean seed. Then open the seed. Use a hand lens to observe what is inside. Can you find the tiny plant?

83

How Pine Trees Grow

Like other plants, most trees grow from seeds. Roots grow down. A green stem grows up. As it grows, the stem becomes woody. The stem of a tree is called a trunk.

When this tree is an adult, it makes cones. The cones hold seeds for new trees. Year after year, more branches and new cones grow. The trunk grows taller and thicker.

Focus Skill **SEQUENCE** **What happens to a pine tree year after year?**

cones

seed sprouting

seedling

adult tree

small tree

Seeds

Seeds may look different, but they are the same in an important way. They all can grow into new plants. The new plant will look like the plant that made the seed.

Where are the seeds in these pictures?

peas

strawberry

sunflower

avocado

pepper

For more links and activities, go to www.hspscience.com

86

1. SEQUENCE Copy and complete this chart.

> **Life Cycle of a Tree**

A _____ hold
B _____.

Roots grow down and a green **C** _____ grows up.

The **D** _____ becomes woody.

The small tree grows into an adult tree.

2. DRAW CONCLUSIONS What is the same about the ways trees and other plants grow? What is different?

3. VOCABULARY Use the words **seed coat** to talk about this picture.

Test Prep

4. What will the plant that grows from a seed be like? How do you know?

Links

Math

Compare Results

Copy the chart. Find out about more plants. Put them in order by how long they live, from shortest life to longest. Which live longer, trees or other plants?

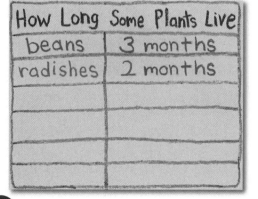

How Long Some Plants Live	
beans	3 months
radishes	2 months

 For more links and activities, go to www.hspscience.com

4

How Can We Group Plants?

Fast Fact

There are many kinds of trees. Each has leaves that look different. You can classify plants by ways they are alike and different.

Classify Leaves

You need

● **6 leaves**

● **index cards**

Step 1

Compare the leaves.
Do you see any patterns?
Classify them into
two groups.

Step 2

Use index cards to make
labels for the groups.

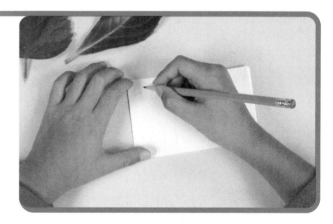

Step 3

Tell how you classified
your leaves.

Inquiry Skill

When you **classify**, you
put things into groups by
ways they are alike.

VOCABULARY	**READING FOCUS SKILL**
edible	**COMPARE AND CONTRAST** Look for ways
nonedible	plants are alike and different.

Grouping Plants

One way to group plants is by looking at their parts. Grasses are one kind of plant. They all have long, thin leaves. They also have very small flowers. You often do not see the flowers. They get cut off when you cut the grass.

flower

grass

Trees and shrubs are groups of plants. They both have woody stems. Most trees have one big main stem. Shrubs have many smaller stems. Some trees and shrubs may have flowers, too.

tree

★ **COMPARE AND CONTRAST**
How are these plants alike and different?

shrub

Plants You Can Eat

You can group plants by whether they are safe to eat. **Edible** things are safe to eat. Some kinds of plants that have edible parts are tomatoes, onions, and squash.

What edible plants can you get at this market?

Plants you cannot eat safely are **nonedible** plants. The flowers below are nonedible plants.

Insta-Lab

Looking at Lunch

Observe your lunch. Draw a picture of it. Label the parts that come from plants. What are some kinds of plants you eat?

★ **COMPARE AND CONTRAST**
Focus Skill

What is the difference between edible plants and nonedible plants?

93

Ways We Use Plants

You can group plants by their uses. People use cotton to make clothing. They use trees to make houses and toys.

⭐ **COMPARE AND CONTRAST**
How are cotton plants and trees alike?

cotton

cotton shirt

wooden toy

pine tree

94

1. COMPARE AND CONTRAST Copy and complete this chart.

Trees and Shrubs

alike

Both have **Ⓐ** _____ stems.

different

Most **Ⓑ** _____ have one big main stem.

Ⓒ _____ have many smaller stems.

2. SUMMARIZE Write sentences to summarize the lesson.

3. VOCABULARY Use the word **edible** to talk about this picture.

Test Prep

4. Which plant do many people use to make clothing?

    A. cotton
    B. grass
    C. pine tree
    D. shrub

Social Studies

Plant Product Collage

Cut out pictures of things people get from plants. Make groups of food, clothing, and things from a home. Glue the pictures onto a sheet of paper.

 For more links and activities, go to www.hspscience.com

Late Bloomers

William Beal was a scientist. He lived about 125 years ago in Michigan. He put sand and seeds in 20 bottles. Then he buried the bottles in the ground.

Beal wanted to see if the seeds could still grow after being buried for a long time. The seeds were kept dry and dark so they would not grow.

Every 20 Years

Beal planned to dig up one bottle every five years. Over time, that was changed to every 20 years. A bottle was dug up in April 2000.

People dug up the bottle and planted the seeds. 26 of the 1,000 seeds grew into bright yellow flowers.

Important Work

The study helps people learn about soil and plants. It shows why weeds can grow in a plowed field. The work also helps scientists learn how seeds can live through fires and floods.

THINK ABOUT IT

Why was it important to keep the seeds in a dry, dark place?

Find out more! Log on to
www.hspscience.com

THE Plant DOCTOR

George Washington Carver was a plant scientist. Some people called him "the plant doctor." Carver worked with farmers who grew crops. He showed them how to plant peanuts to keep their soil healthy.

Carver thought of 300 things to make with peanut plants! Can you imagine washing your hair with shampoo made from peanuts? He also made foods, medicines, soaps, paints, rubber, gasoline, and paper—all from the peanut plant.

You Can Do It!

Investigate Different Plants' Needs

What to Do

1. Do all plants need exactly the same things? Get three plants. Plan an investigation to answer the question.

2. Follow your plan.

3. Draw pictures and write sentences to record what happens.

Materials
- 3 different kinds of plants

Draw Conclusions

Did you answer the question? If not, how could you change your investigation?

How Seeds Get Around

Wind, water, and animals move seeds from place to place. Get different seeds or pictures of seeds. Observe each seed. Then find out what kind of seed it is and how it is moved. Use books and other resources.

Review and Test Preparation

Vocabulary Review

Look at the numbers next to the plant parts in the picture. Tell the number and the name of each part.

roots p. 75   **flowers** p. 78

stem p. 76   **fruits** p. 78

leaves p. 77   **seeds** p. 78

Check Understanding

7. What happens to a plant that gets air, light, water, and nutrients? Tell how you know.

8. You can eat corn. Which group does it belong in?

  A. edible plants   **C.** water

  B. nonedible plants **D.** trees

Critical Thinking

Over time, Hayden observes this tree in her back yard.

9. What is happening in each picture?

10. Predict what will happen to this tree next year. Tell how you know.

Chapter 3

Environments for Living Things

Vocabulary

environment
adaptation
camouflage
oxygen
pollen
food chain

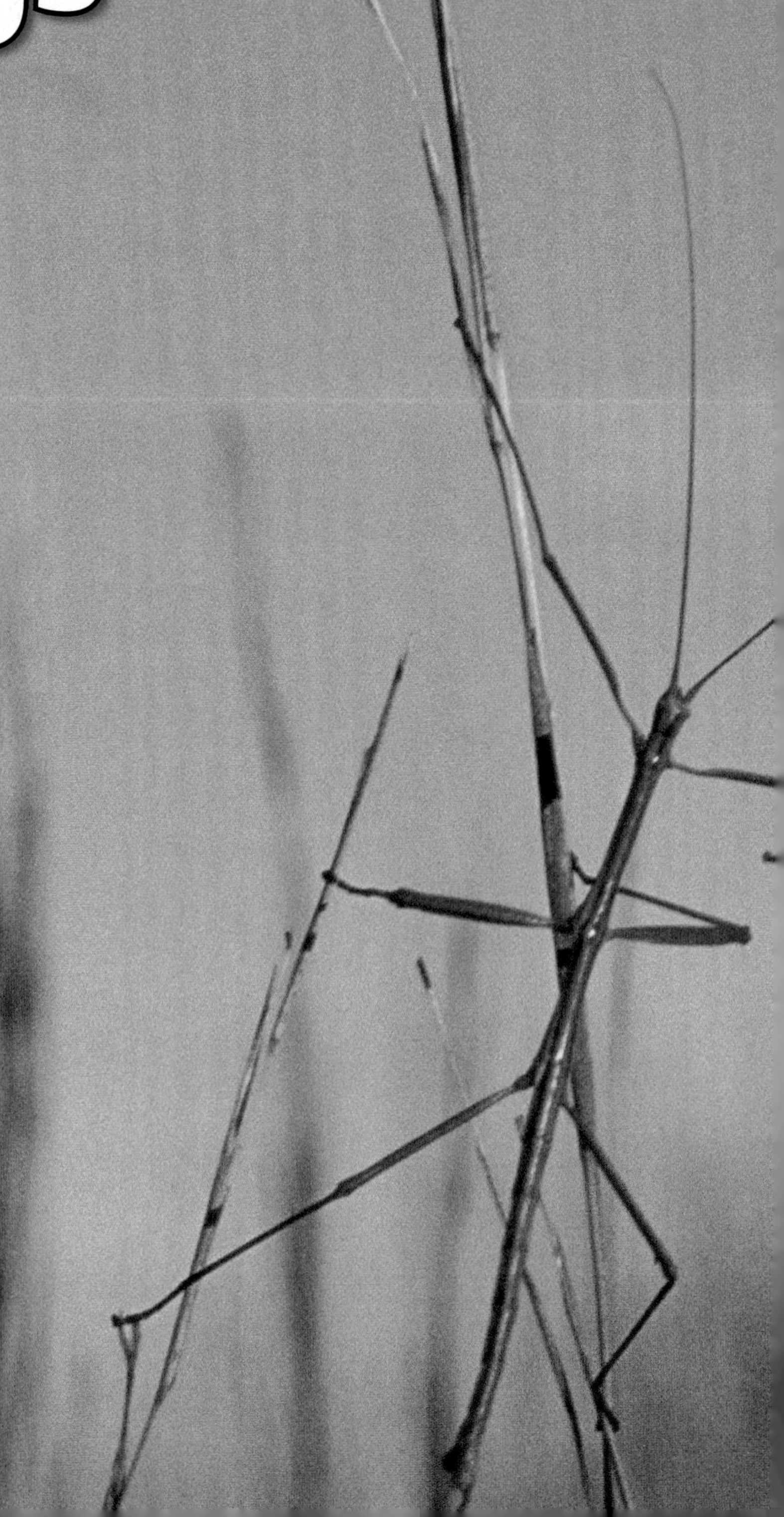

I wonder...

Why do these insects look like plants?

What do **YOU** wonder?

What Is an Environment?

Fast Fact

Few people have ever seen jaguars in the wild. They live where it is easy to hide. Communicate what you know about where animals live.

Where Animals Live

You need

- animal picture cards
- crayons

Step 1

Look at the cards. Choose an animal you know about.

Step 2

Draw the animal where it lives.

Step 3

Communicate with classmates about what you drew.

Inquiry Skill

When you **communicate**, you tell about each thing you drew in your picture.

 **READING FOCUS SKILL**

MAIN IDEA AND DETAILS Look for the main ideas about environments.

Environments

An **environment** is made up of all the things in a place.

An environment has living things. It has plants and animals.

Find living and nonliving things in this environment.

An environment also has nonliving things, such as rocks and water.

⭐ **MAIN IDEA AND DETAILS**
What is an environment?

Insta-Lab

Living	Nonliving
grass	soil
birds	rocks
ants	air

Environments Near You

Go on a nature walk with your class. Observe the environment. What living things do you see? What nonliving things do you see? Make two lists.

People and Environments

People can change environments. They may build houses and roads. They may make new things. People made many of the things you see in your environment.

⭐ **MAIN IDEA AND DETAILS** How can people change environments?

Which things here did people make? Which things were not made by people?

1. MAIN IDEA AND DETAILS Copy and complete this chart.

Main Idea
An Ⓐ _____ is all the things in a place.

detail	detail	detail
People can Ⓑ _____ it.	It has living things.	It has Ⓒ _____ things.

2. SUMMARIZE Use the chart to write a lesson summary.

3. VOCABULARY Tell about this animal's **environment**.

Test Prep
4. Tell about some ways people can change their environments.

Writing

Write a Description
Look at the environment outside your school. Write sentences about things you see that were made by people. Tell what each thing looks like. Tell what it is used for.

The slide was made by people. It is red and blue. It is for kids to play on.

For more links and activities, go to www.hspscience.com

Lesson 2

What Helps Plants and Animals Live in Places?

Fast Fact

An alligator has eyes on the top of its head. Draw a conclusion about how this might help an alligator.

Some Animals Hide

You need

- colored paper clips
- colored paper

Step 1

Put the clips on a sheet of colored paper. Which clips are hard to see?

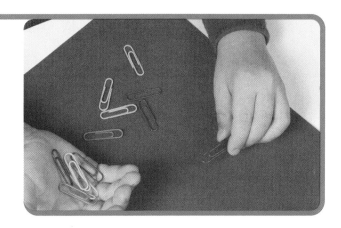

Step 2

Put the clips on a sheet of paper of a different color. Which clips are hard to see now?

Step 3

Draw a conclusion about how color helps some animals hide.

Inquiry Skill

To **draw a conclusion** about animals' colors, think about the clips that were hard to see.

111

READING FOCUS SKILL

COMPARE AND CONTRAST Look for ways adaptations are alike and different.

Plant Adaptations

An **adaptation** is a body part or a behavior that helps a living thing.

Plants have adaptations. Some adaptations help them get water. A banyan tree has many roots. A jade plant has thick leaves that store water.

banyan tree

jade plant

112

Some adaptations help plants stay alive. Bark protects trees. Thorns on plants stop animals from eating them. Other adaptations help plants make new plants. Wings on maple seeds carry the seeds to new places. Flowers attract small animals. The animals help the plants make seeds.

maple seeds

COMPARE AND CONTRAST What are some plant adaptations? How are they alike and different?

hummingbird

rose

Animal Adaptations

Animals have adaptations, too. Some adaptations help animals eat. Sharp teeth help a lion bite meat. A long tongue helps an anteater get ants.

Some adaptations help animals move. Fins help a fish swim. Wings and feathers help a bird fly.

scarlet ibis

lion

anteater

Some adaptations keep animals safe. A porcupine has sharp quills. Other animals keep away from the quills.

★ **COMPARE AND CONTRAST**
Focus Skill
How are some animal adaptations alike?

Insta-Lab

Observe Beaks
Put crumbs from lunch on a tray. Put the tray outside where you can see it. Then watch for birds. What birds do you see? How does each one use its beak to eat?

goldfish

porcupine

115

Camouflage

Some animals have an adaptation called camouflage. **Camouflage** is a color or pattern that helps an animal hide. Animals need to hide to stay safe or to find food.

arctic fox in winter

arctic fox in summer

flounder

dead-leaf butterfly

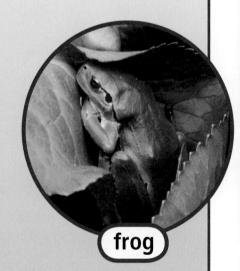

frog

 For more links and activities, go to www.hspscience.com

1. COMPARE AND CONTRAST Copy and complete this chart.

Adaptation

alike

Ⓐ _____ help living things.

different

Some help plants get Ⓑ _____.

Some help plants stay alive or Ⓒ _____.

Some help animals Ⓓ _____.

Some help Ⓔ _____ move.

Some help animals stay Ⓕ _____.

2. DRAW CONCLUSIONS Why do you think some animals have camouflage?

3. VOCABULARY Use the word **adaptation** to tell about this picture.

Test Prep

4. Which adaptation helps plants store water?
   A. flowers
   B. sharp teeth
   C. thick leaves
   D. thorns

Links

Math

Counting Teeth

Some animals have many teeth. Others do not. How many teeth do you have? Use a mirror to count. Use the data to make a class graph. Does everyone have the same number of teeth?

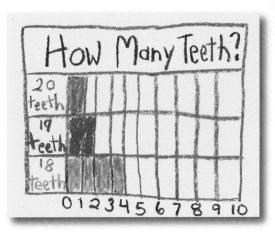

 For more links and activities, go to www.hspscience.com

Lesson 3

How Do Plants and Animals Need Each Other?

Fast Fact

Flowers make food that bees eat. Bees carry pollen, which helps plants make new plants. What else can you observe about plants and animals?

118

Animals in a Tree

You need

● **hand lens**

Step 1

Find a tree with your class. **Observe** it with a hand lens. Record what you see.

Step 2

Sit quietly and **observe**. Record what animals in your tree are doing.

Step 3

How did animals use the tree? Talk about what you **observed**.

Inquiry Skill

Use your senses to help you **observe**.

VOCABULARY

oxygen
pollen
food chain

 READING FOCUS SKILL

MAIN IDEA AND DETAILS Look for the main ideas about how animals use plants and help plants.

Animals Use Plants

Animals use plants to meet their needs. Some live in plants or use them to make homes. Plants are good places for animals to hide in, too.

heron hiding in grass

deer hiding behind trees

beaver building a dam

120

Some animals use plants for food. Animals need to breathe oxygen from the air. **Oxygen** is a kind of gas. Plants put oxygen into the air.

⭐ **MAIN IDEA AND DETAILS**
What are three ways animals use plants?

Insta-Lab

Homes from Plants

Some birds use plant parts and mud to make nests. Use twigs, grass, and clay to make a model of a bird's nest.

elephants eating leaves

Animals Help Plants

Some animals help plants make new plants. They carry **pollen** from flower to flower. Pollen is a powder that flowers need to make seeds.

honey possum carrying pollen

butterfly carrying pollen

Some animals help plants by carrying seeds. They take seeds to new places. The seeds may grow into new plants there.

⭐ **MAIN IDEA AND DETAILS**
Focus Skill
How can animals help plants make new plants?

squirrel carrying seeds

dog carrying seeds

123

Food Chain

Animals can be grouped by what they eat. Some animals eat plants. Some eat other animals. A **food chain** shows how animals and plants are linked.

⭐ (Focus Skill) **MAIN IDEA AND DETAILS**
What does a food chain show?

Last, a bear eats the fish.

Next, a rainbow trout eats the stonefly.

First, a stonefly eats part of a plant.

124

1. MAIN IDEA AND DETAILS Copy and complete this chart.

Main Idea
Animals and plants need each other.

detail	detail	detail	detail
Animals eat **Ⓐ** _____.	Animals carry **Ⓑ** _____ from flower to flower.	Animals use plants for **Ⓒ** _____.	Animals carry **Ⓓ** _____ to new places.

2. SUMMARIZE Write two sentences to summarize the lesson.

3. VOCABULARY Use the word **pollen** to tell about this animal.

Test Prep

4. Which of these shows how animals are linked?
- **A.** air
- **B.** environment
- **C.** flowers
- **D.** food chain

Links

 Social Studies

You Need Plants and Animals
How do you use plants and animals to meet your needs? Draw pictures and write sentences to show the ways. Put your pages together to make a book.

💻 **For more links and activities, go to www.hspscience.com**

Now You See It, Now You Don't

Do you ever wish you could hide like an arctic fox? Now your wish can come true.

Susumu Tachi is a teacher. He lives in Japan. Tachi made a coat to show how things can be hidden.

Tiny Glass Beads

The coat is covered by many tiny glass beads. The beads reflect light. Then you can see through a person wearing the coat.

THINK ABOUT IT

How is this coat similar to camouflage?

Seeing into the Future

Tachi says his idea might be used in many ways. Doctors could use tools with the beads on them. Then they could see through the tools when they operate.

Find out more! Log on to **www.hspscience.com**

Where Are All the Butterflies?

People often see monarch butterflies in the fall. The insects leave places in the north when the weather turns cold. They fly to warmer places in the south. Scientists want to know why.

Emma Griffiths helped scientists count butterflies. Emma helped by scooping up butterflies. Then scientists put a tiny tag on each insect. The tag showed other scientists that the butterflies came from Connecticut.

You Can Do It!

What Makes Seeds Stick?

What to Do

1. Find some seeds. Which ones might stick to animals?

2. Make a model of a seed that will stick to things.

3. Does your model stick to your clothes? How does this help you understand how seeds stick to animals?

Materials
- foam ball
- glue
- rough materials

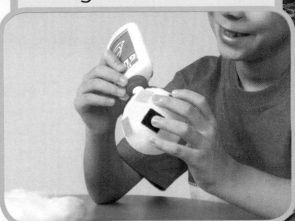

Draw Conclusions

How is the ball a model of a seed that sticks to things?

Watch a Plant Change

Put two plants that are the same by a window. Mark one. Each day, turn the other plant. Do not turn the marked plant. After one week, how has the marked plant changed? Why did it do this?

Review and Test Preparation

Vocabulary Review

Choose the best word to complete each sentence.

environment p. 106   **oxygen** p. 121

camouflage p. 116   **pollen** p. 122

1. Powder from flowers is ____.

2. A gas that is part of air is ____.

3. An adaptation that helps an animal hide is ____.

4. A place that is made up of living and nonliving things is an ____.

Check Understanding

5. Name two animals. Tell how the adaptations of these animals are **alike**. Then tell how they are **different**.

6. How do plants help animals breathe?

    A. Plants put oxygen into the air.

    B. Animals eat plants.

    C. Plants store water.

    D. Animals can hide in plants.

Critical Thinking

7. Why do you think people change their environments? How do some changes harm the plants and animals that live there?

8. Look at these plants and animals. Draw them in order to show a food chain. Write about what happens.

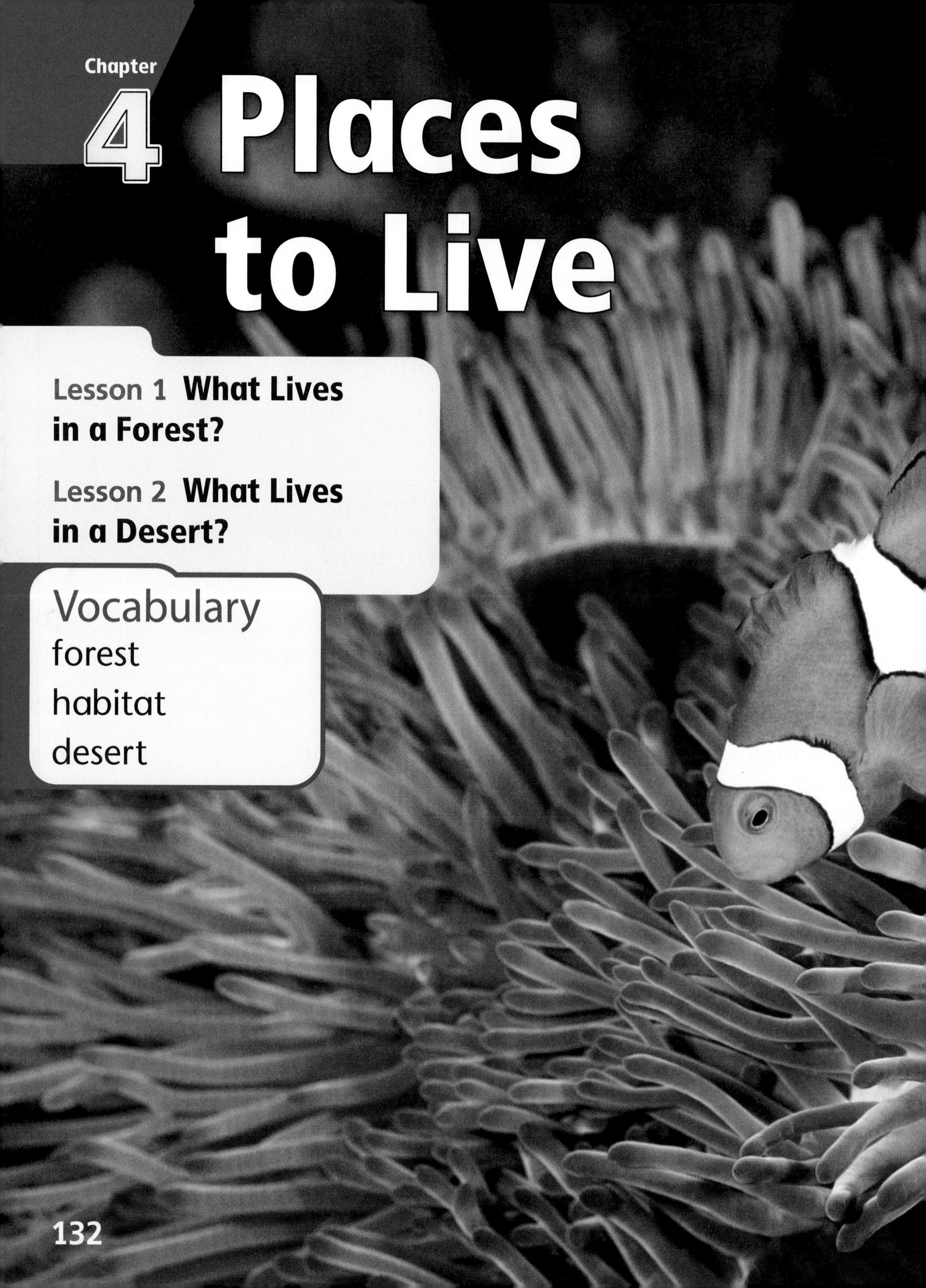

Chapter

4 Places to Live

Lesson 1 **What Lives in a Forest?**

Lesson 2 **What Lives in a Desert?**

Vocabulary

forest

habitat

desert

I wonder...

Why does this fish live here?

What do **YOU** wonder?

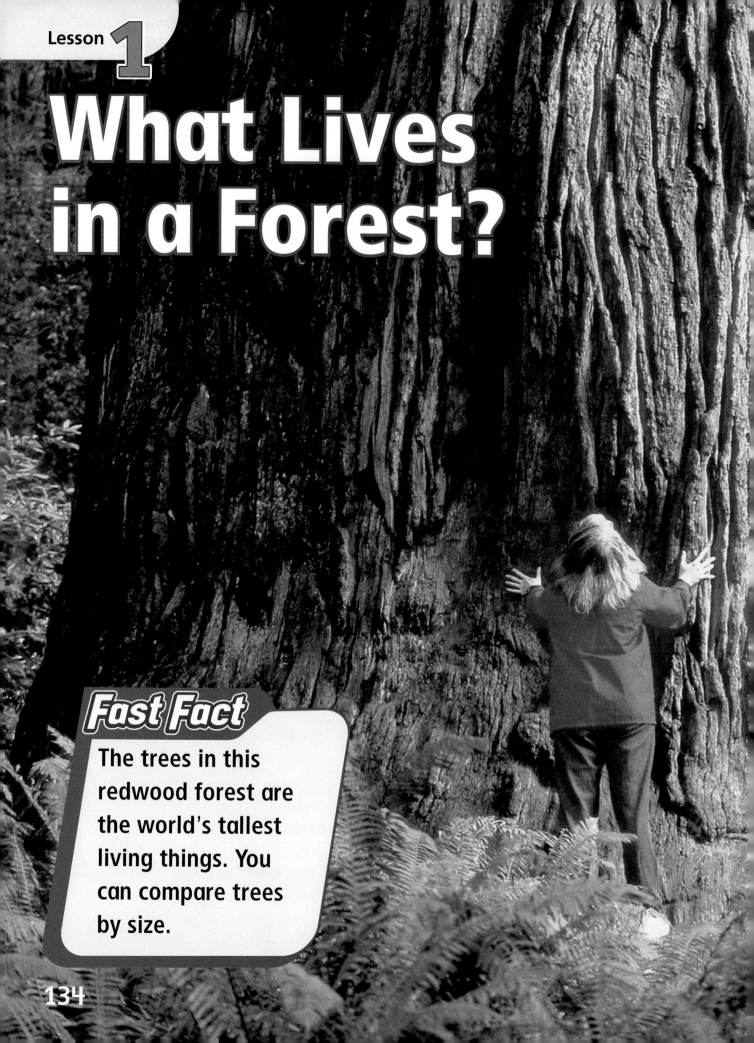

What Lives in a Forest?

Fast Fact

The trees in this redwood forest are the world's tallest living things. You can compare trees by size.

Compare Leaves and Bark

You need

- **dark-colored crayon**
- **paper**

Step 1

Go outside with your class. Find a leaf. Make a rubbing.

Step 2

Find the tree that the leaf is from. Make a rubbing of its bark.

Step 3

Compare your rubbings with a classmate's rubbings. Tell what you see.

Inquiry Skill

When you **compare**, you look for ways things are alike and ways they are different.

READING FOCUS SKILL

MAIN IDEA AND DETAILS Look for the main ideas about forests.

Forests

A **forest** is land that is covered with trees. The trees shade the forest floor. The shade helps the soil stay moist.

 MAIN IDEA AND DETAILS **What is a forest?**

Forest Plants

In a forest, trees get enough rain and warmth to grow tall. Their leaves can get the light they need. Ferns and flowers grow on the forest floor. They need water, but they do not need much light.

ferns

MAIN IDEA AND DETAILS
How do trees get the light they need?

wildflowers

Made in the Shade

Wet two paper towels. Put them in a sunny place. Use a folder to make shade for one towel. Wait a few minutes. Then check the towels. Which one is wetter? How is the wetter towel like a forest floor?

137

Forest Animals

A forest has habitats for many animals. A **habitat** is a place where an animal finds food, water, and shelter. A bear needs a large part of a forest for its habitat. A smaller animal may need only a log.

eagle

⭐ **MAIN IDEA AND DETAILS**
Focus Skill

What are some animals that may have habitats in a forest?

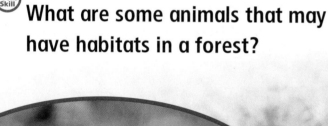

skunk

bear

How are these animals meeting their needs?

1. MAIN IDEA AND DETAILS Copy and complete this chart.

Forest

Main Idea
A Ⓐ ＿＿＿ is a place where many trees grow.

details
Trees get enough rain and
Ⓑ ＿＿＿.
Ferns and forest flowers do not need much Ⓒ ＿＿＿.

details
Bears need a large part of the Ⓓ ＿＿＿ to live in.
Smaller animals may live in a Ⓔ ＿＿＿ in the forest.

2. SUMMARIZE Use the chart to write a lesson summary.

3. VOCABULARY
Use the words **forest** and **habitat** to tell about this picture.

Test Prep
4. Why could a log be a good habitat for a small animal?

Links

Writing

Write a Story
Write a story about a forest animal. Tell where it lives, what it eats, and what it does. Draw pictures that show the animal in the forest.

This bear lives in the forest with her mom and her brother.

For more links and activities, go to www.hspscience.com

139

What Lives in a Desert?

Fast Fact

A barrel cactus can live for almost 6 years on water stored in its stem. You can draw a conclusion about why some plants can live in deserts.

Desert Plants

You need

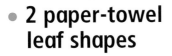 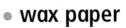 

- 2 paper-towel leaf shapes
- water
- wax paper
- 2 paper clips

Step 1

Make the leaf shapes damp. Fold the wax paper. Put one leaf inside the fold. Clip it.

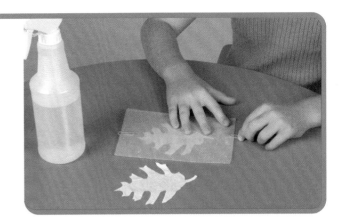

Step 2

Put the leaf shapes in a sunny place. Observe them in one hour.

Step 2

Which leaf was still damp? Why?
Draw a conclusion.

Inquiry Skill

Think about what you know about wax paper and water to **draw a conclusion**.

VOCABULARY
desert

 READING FOCUS SKILL

MAIN IDEA AND DETAILS Look for the main ideas about deserts.

Deserts

A **desert** is land that gets very little rain. Most deserts are sunny all year long. The soil is very dry. Only some plants or animals can live there.

MAIN IDEA AND DETAILS How can you tell if a place is a desert?

creosote

142

Desert Plants

Desert plants do not need much water. A cactus is a desert plant. It can hold water in its thick stem. Its waxy covering helps keep water in.

 **MAIN IDEA AND DETAILS** How does a cactus live without much water?

brittlebush

Insta-Lab

Soak It Up

Get a sponge that is very dry. Put water on it a little at a time. Observe the sponge. How does it change? How is the sponge like the stem of a cactus?

143

Desert Animals

Desert animals need to keep cool and find water. The dove and the hare rest in shady places. The tortoise gets water from its food.

desert hare

white-winged dove

How are these animals meeting their needs?

desert tortoise

 For more links and activities, go to www.hspscience.com

144

1. MAIN IDEA AND DETAILS Copy and complete this chart.

Desert

Main Idea
A desert is land that gets very little **A** _____.

details
Desert plants do not need much **B** _____.
A cactus holds water in its **C** _____.

details
Doves and hares rest in **D** _____ places to stay cool.
A **E** _____ gets water from the food it eats.

2. DRAW CONCLUSIONS Why are few plants and animals able to live in a desert?

3. VOCABULARY Use the word **desert** to tell about this picture.

Test Prep

4. Which word best describes a desert?
- **A.** cloudy
- **B.** cool
- **C.** dry
- **D.** wet

Links

Math

Measure Rainfall
Deserts get less than 25 centimeters of rain each year. How much rain falls where you live? Measure that amount and 25 centimeters on a sheet of paper. Compare.

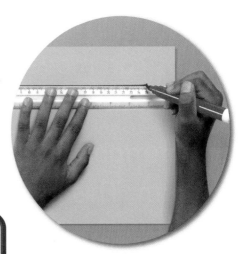

 For more links and activities, go to **www.hspscience.com**

A New Plane Fights Fires

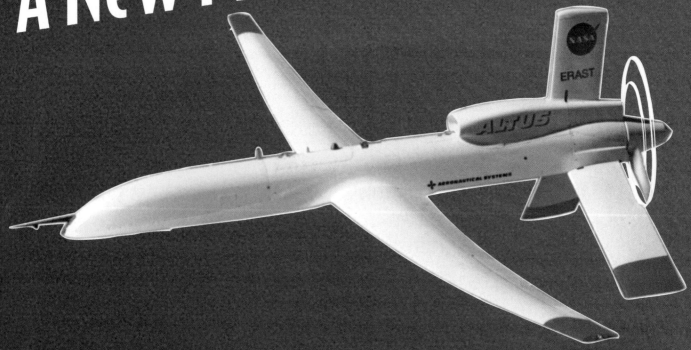

Wildfires burn large parts of forests in the western United States. Wildfires can move quickly. This can put firefighters in danger.

Now firefighters have a new tool to help them. This tool is a robot plane called Altus II.

Plane Without a Pilot

Altus II is 17 meters (55 feet) across. It can fly at about 185 kilometers (115 miles) per hour. The plane does not have a pilot. It is controlled by people on the ground.

The Altus II has cameras on board. It takes pictures of fires. The cameras can see through smoke. They can also see places that might catch fire.

The plane can also be used by people to keep track of floods or hurricanes.

THINK ABOUT IT
How does using Altus II help firefighters?

All in a Day's Work

The Altus II is light. It does not need much fuel. It can fly for up to 24 hours at a time.

Spin-In Find out more! Log on to **www.hspscience.com**

A Walk in the Woods

What lives in a forest? Andrew Seto found out when his class went for a walk in the woods near his school.

Andrew knows that plants live in a forest. He saw oak trees and ferns.

Andrew knows that birds make their homes in trees. He saw that squirrels make their homes in trees, too.

You Can Do It!

Fish Habitat

What to Do

1. Put rocks in the bottom of a fishbowl or an aquarium. Fill it with water. Put in two or more fish.
2. Feed the fish every day. Keep the habitat clean.
3. Observe and record what you see each day.

Materials
- fishbowl with water
- aquarium rocks
- fish

Draw Conclusions

How do fish in a pond get food?

Deserts Around the World

Find pictures of deserts in other parts of the world. Observe the land and the plants and animals that live there. How are these deserts like American deserts? How are they different? Draw pictures to show what you find out. Write about them.

Camels live in deserts in the Middle East.

Review and Test Preparation

Vocabulary Review

Use the words below to complete the sentences.

forest p. 136   **desert** p. 142

habitat p. 138

1. A place where an animal can find food, water, and shelter is a ____.

2. Land that is covered with trees is a ____.

3. Land that gets little rain is a ____.

Check Understanding

4. **Compare** these animals' habitats.

5. Why is a forest a good habitat for this skunk?

    A. A forest is very dry.

    B. The skunk can live without much water.

    C. The skunk likes the sun.

    D. The skunk can find food and shelter.

6. Where does a tortoise get water?

    F. from a lake

    G. from its food

    H. from the rain

    J. from a stream

Critical Thinking

7. Read the clues. Name the plant or animal. Tell where it lives.

This plant needs rain and warmth to grow. It grows tall so that its leaves can get light.

8. Write clues about a plant or animal from this chapter. Ask a partner to name your plant or animal.

151

High Desert Plants

Bisbee

Do you like cactus plants? If you do, you'll love the Arizona Cactus and Succulent Research Center. You can see lots of cactuses there.

There are 800 kinds of desert plants at the center. All of these plants are succulents.

A succulent is a plant with thick stems or branches that store water. This extra water helps the plant live in the desert.

A cactus is a succulent.

Spring is here!

A Close Look at a Cactus

A cactus is one kind of succulent plant.

Some cactuses have spines, or thorns, on their stems and branches.

The spines are sharp. They protect the cactus from animals who may try to eat it. Some also cover the cactus enough to keep it cool.

Many animals like to make their homes on or in a cactus. If you look carefully, you might see one!

Look, a nest!

Think and Do

1. SCIENTIFIC THINKING Why does a cactus store water in its stem? How does the water get there? Draw a picture that shows how water might get inside a cactus.

2. SCIENCE AND TECHNOLOGY Use books or the Internet to find out where else cactus plants can grow in the United States. Find out about different kinds of cactuses. Draw pictures of them, and write sentences telling where they grow in the United States.

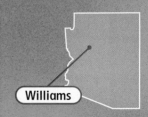

Williams

Grand Canyon Deer Farm

At the Grand Canyon Deer Farm, you can do more than look at deer. You can walk with them and touch them. You can even let them eat from your hand.

There are many kinds of deer at the farm. There are even reindeer from Alaska!

Reach out and touch a deer!

154

Where the Animals Roam

The Deer Farm is part of a zoo. At the zoo, you can meet lots of different animals.

There are antelopes, wallabies, llamas, chickens, turkeys, goats, peacocks, a pig, and a buffalo. There are even two talking birds.

You can have fun here while you learn about the animals. The zoo is a safe place for them to live and grow up.

Come visit the zoo. There are lots of animals waiting to meet you!

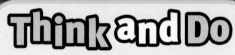

Think and Do

1. SCIENTIFIC THINKING Choose two of the animals who live at Deer Farm. Think about where they live in the zoo. How are their homes the same? How are they different? Draw a picture of each animal's home at the zoo.

2. SCIENCE AND TECHNOLOGY Scientists use computers to keep track of the animals that live in zoos. What kind of information do you think they keep on the computer about these animals? Make a list of the things you would keep track of on your computer if you were looking after the animals in a zoo.

Meet Our State's Bird

The Arizona state bird is the cactus wren. A cactus wren has brown and white spots and a curved beak.

The cactus wren is a very busy bird. It builds lots of nests, but it only lays eggs in one of them. The other nests keep animals away from the one with the eggs.

Say hello to our state's bird!

What a Nest!

If you look carefully, you may see a nest on an "arm" of a giant cactus. Cactus wrens build their nests high on cholla or saguaro cactuses.

This is a safe place to build a nest. The cactus's sharp spines protect the wren's eggs from animals that would eat them.

The nest is shaped like a football. The wren makes it out of grass, fur, and plants and lines it with feathers. The feathers make it soft inside for the baby birds.

Think and Do

1. SCIENCE AND TECHNOLOGY Suppose you are a cactus wren and you want to build a nest. Where can you build your nest so it will be safe from other animals? Use words and pictures to describe how you would build your nest to keep your eggs safe.

2. SCIENTIFIC THINKING Learn more about our state's bird. How is it like other birds? How is it different? Draw a picture of the cactus wren, and write sentences that tell what is special about it.

157

Compare Growth

Materials
- books about plants and animals
- paper
- ruler
- markers

Procedure
1. Draw a line across a sheet of paper. Make marks on the line for each year of your life. Number them.
2. Draw a picture at each mark. Show how tall you were at that age.
3. Make a chart to show how a palo verde tree grows.
4. Compare the charts.

Draw Conclusions
1. Which grows faster, you or the tree?
2. Which will grow taller?

A Habitat Diorama

Materials
- empty shoe box
- scissors
- tape or glue
- old magazines with pictures of animals
- construction paper
- string

Procedure

1. Choose an animal common to Arizona, such as a cactus wren or a roadrunner. Find pictures and cut them out. (Ask before you cut them out.)
2. Now list the things this animal needs to live. For example, a cactus wren needs a cactus to make its nest in.
3. Make a diorama of the animal and its environment. Show the things that every animal needs in order to survive—shelter, food, and water. Explain your diorama to the class.

Draw Conclusions

1. How might making a list of things that animals need to survive help you protect animals in the wild?
2. How does making a model help you understand what animals need?

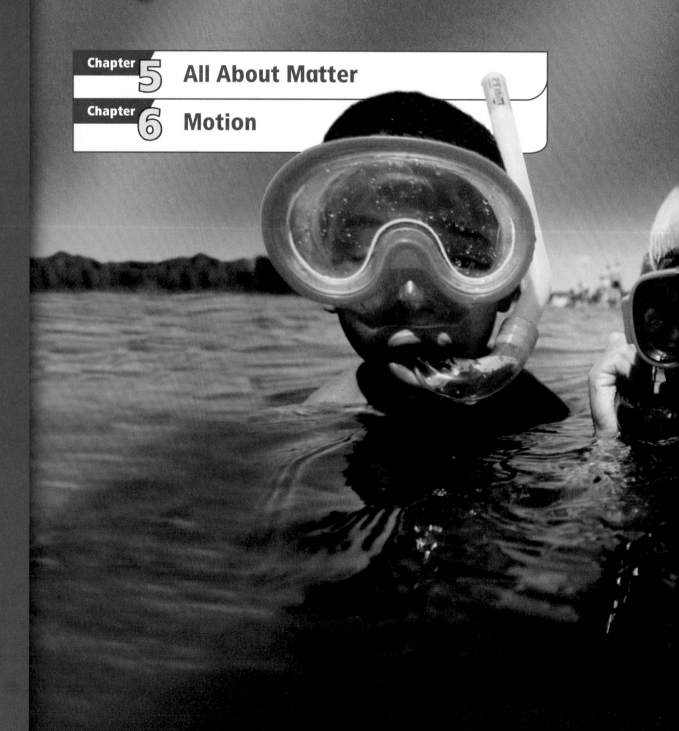

UNIT B

Physical Science

| Chapter 5 | All About Matter |
| Chapter 6 | Motion |

160

Lake Powell

TO: wendy@hspscience.com
FROM: ben@hspscience2.com
RE: Boating

Dear Aunt Wendy,
At school I am learning about solids and liquids. I told my class about your boat. Jumping into the water is fun. Maybe I can visit you this weekend. We can take the boat to Lake Powell.
Your nephew,
Ben

Gravity As you do this unit, you will learn about how things move. Plan and do a test. Find out how to make a toy truck go farther when you roll it.

All About Matter

Vocabulary

matter	liquid
solid	dissolve
mixture	float
length	sink
mass	

I wonder...

Why do things filled with air float in water?

What do **YOU** wonder?

163

What Is Matter?

Fast Fact

The largest stuffed bear was 32 feet tall. You can classify toys by size, shape, and color.

Classify Matter

You need

- objects

Step 1

Observe the objects. Compare their sizes, shapes, and colors.

Step 2

Classify the objects in three ways.

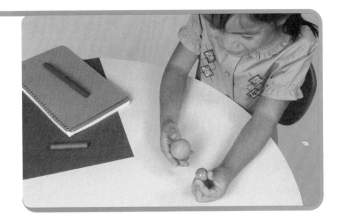

Step 3

Draw pictures of the groups you made.

Inquiry Skill

When you **classify** objects, you sort them by how they are alike.

READING FOCUS SKILL

COMPARE AND CONTRAST Look for ways matter can be alike and different.

Matter

Everything around you is **matter**. Toys are matter. Balloons are matter. Water is matter, too. Some matter has parts that are too hard to see.

> **What matter do you see here?**

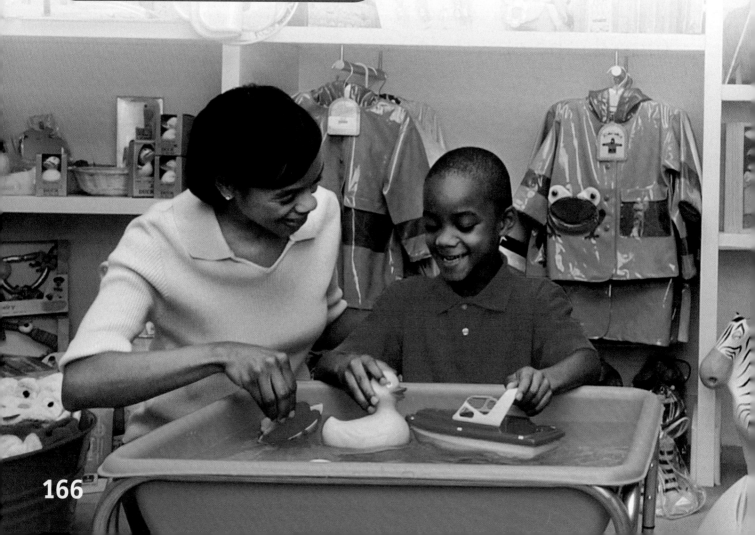

All matter is not the same. Matter can be soft or hard. It can be big or small.

★ Focus Skill **COMPARE AND CONTRAST**
How are the stuffed toy and balloons alike? How are they different?

Insta-Lab

Matter Up Close

Observe sand and soil with a hand lens. How are they alike? How are they different? What does the hand lens help you see? Talk to a partner about what you see.

Sorting Matter

You can sort matter. You can sort these objects by color. You can sort them by shape. How else can you sort them?

⭐ **COMPARE AND CONTRAST**
Focus Skill
How could you sort these objects by color?

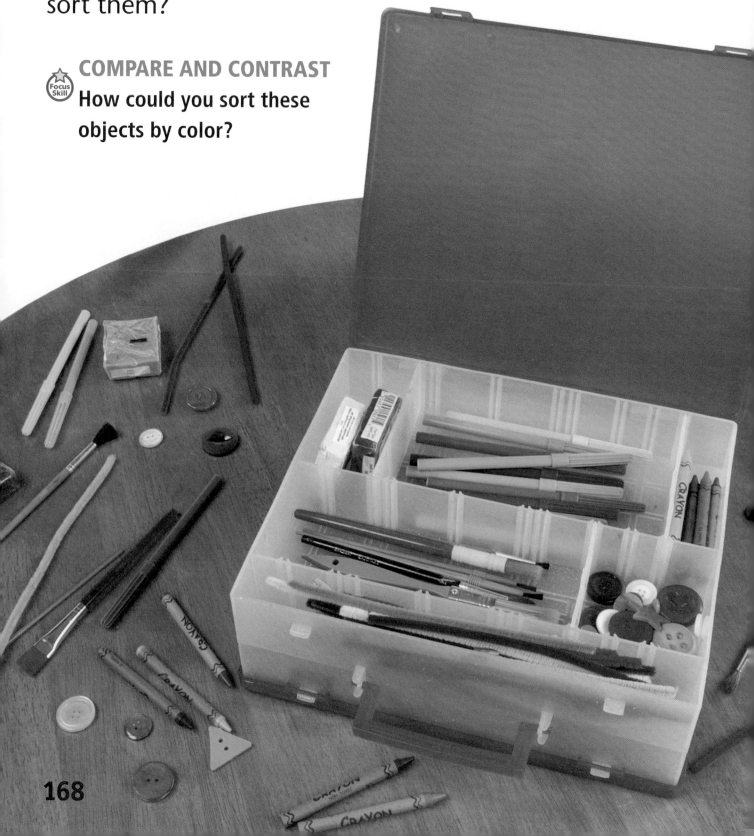

168

1. COMPARE AND CONTRAST Copy and complete this chart.

Matter

alike

A _____ is matter.

different

Matter can be different **B** _____, such as red and yellow.

Matter can be different sizes, such as **C** _____ and **D** _____.

Matter can be different **E** _____, such as circles and squares.

2. SUMMARIZE Write two sentences. Tell how matter can be alike and different.

3. VOCABULARY Tell about the **matter** in this picture.

Test Prep

4. Which is true about matter?
   A. It is all the same color.
   B. It is all the same size.
   C. It is only soft things.
   D. Everything is matter.

Links

Writing

Labeling Matter
Use self-stick notes to make labels for matter in your classroom. On each label, name the matter. Then write three words that tell about it.

book
hard, heavy, purple

pencil
small, yellow, pointed

For more links and activities, go to www.hspscience.com

What Can We Observe About Solids?

Fast Fact

These animals are made of millions of toy blocks. You can compare toys in many ways.

Measuring Mass

You need

- **2 blocks**

- **balance**

Step 1

Put a block on each side of the balance.

Step 2

Look at the blocks on the balance. **Compare**.

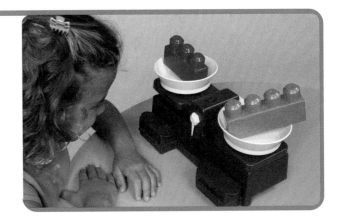

Step 3

Which block has more mass? Which has less mass?

Inquiry Skill

When you **compare** with a balance, you see how much mass things have.

VOCABULARY

solid
mixture
length
mass

READING FOCUS SKILL

MAIN IDEA AND DETAILS Look for the main ideas about solids.

Observing Solids

How are paper, scissors, and a globe the same? They are all solids.

A **solid** is a kind of matter that keeps its shape. It keeps its shape even when you move it.

⭐ **MAIN IDEA AND DETAILS**
How do you know musical instruments are solids?

173

Mixing Solids

When you mix different kinds of matter together, you make a **mixture**. A mixture is made up of two or more things. These drawing tools make a mixture of solids.

The things in a mixture do not change. You can sort them back out of the mixture.

⭐ MAIN IDEA AND DETAILS
Focus Skill

What is a mixture made up of?

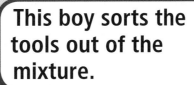

This boy sorts the tools out of the mixture.

Make Mixtures

Get small things from the classroom. Mix them together. Then trade mixtures with a partner. Sort the things back out of each other's mixtures.

175

Measuring Solids

You can measure solids. You can measure how long a solid is. That is its **length**. You measure length with a ruler.

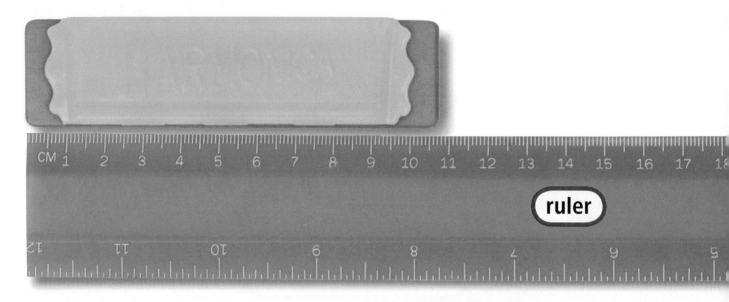

ruler

You can measure the mass of a solid. **Mass** is the amount of matter a solid has. You measure mass with a balance.

MAIN IDEA AND DETAILS What are two ways you can measure solids?

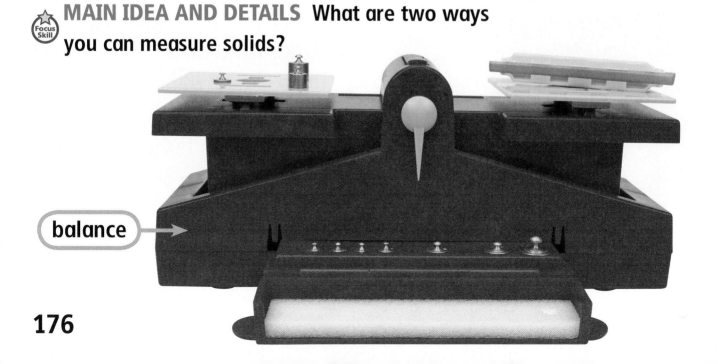

balance

1. MAIN IDEA AND DETAILS Copy and complete this chart.

> **Solids**

> **Main Idea**
> A solid is matter that keeps its shape.

> **detail**
> You can mix solids.

> **detail**
> You can Ⓐ _____ solids.

2. DRAW CONCLUSIONS
How do you know a pencil is a solid?

3. VOCABULARY Tell about the **mass** of these blocks.

Test Prep
4. Write a sentence about two solids you see. Tell how they are alike.

Links

Math

Measure Length
Find three small objects in your classroom. Use paper clips to measure their lengths. Record the lengths in a bar graph. Which object is the longest?

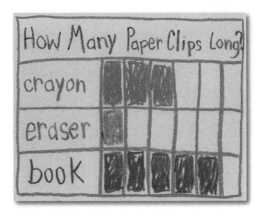

 For more links and activities, go to www.hspscience.com

What Can We Observe About Liquids?

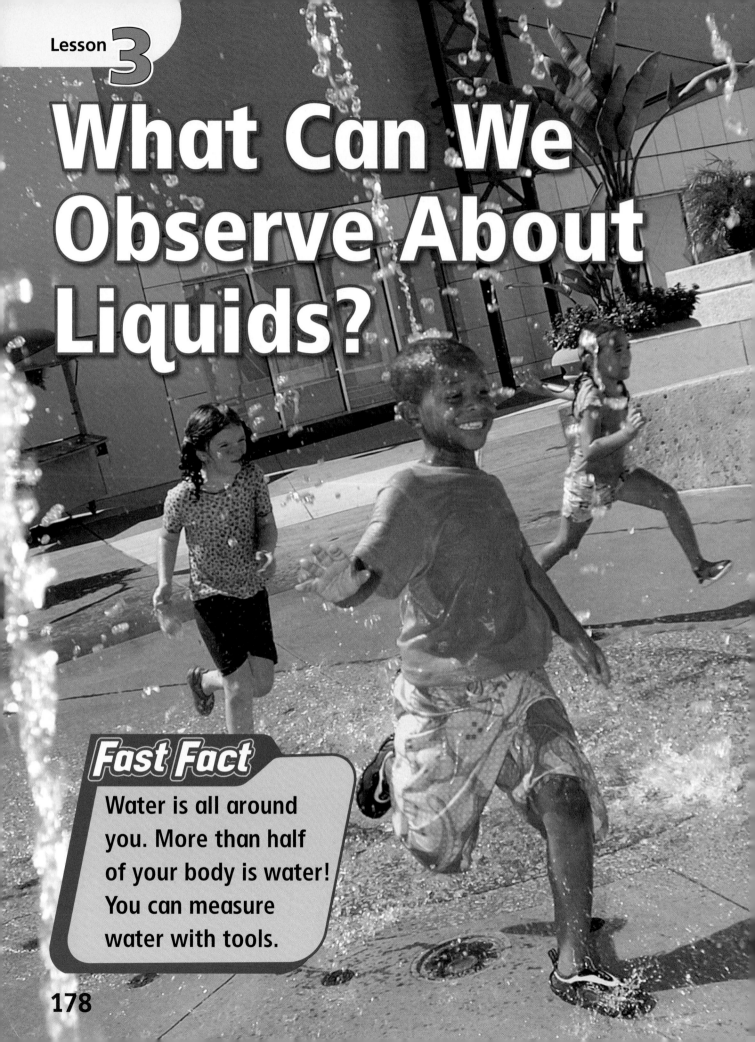

Fast Fact

Water is all around you. More than half of your body is water! You can measure water with tools.

The Shape of Liquids

You need

- **3 containers of water**
- **measuring cup**

Step 1

Look at the containers. Draw their shapes.

Step 2

Predict which container will have the most water.

Step 3

Measure the water in each container. Was your prediction right?

Inquiry Skill

When you **measure** something, you use tools to learn about it.

Reading in Science

VOCABULARY
liquid
dissolve
float
sink

 READING FOCUS SKILL

MAIN IDEA AND DETAILS Look for main ideas about liquids.

Observing Liquids

How are the soap and water alike? Both are liquids.

A **liquid** is matter that flows. It does not have its own shape. It takes the shape of its container.

 MAIN IDEA AND DETAILS
What is a liquid?

liquid soap

water

Liquid Mixtures

You can make mixtures with liquids. You can mix drink powder or salt with water. They **dissolve**, or mix completely with the liquid.

If you mix soil or oil with water, they do not dissolve.

⭐ **MAIN IDEA AND DETAILS** How can you tell if something dissolves?

Mix	Do Not Mix
juice	soil
salt	oil

Float and Sink

Does matter float or sink?
You can test it.

Some objects **float**, or
stay on top of a liquid.

Which objects sink?

Some objects **sink**, or fall to the bottom of a liquid.

★ **MAIN IDEA AND DETAILS** How can you find out if matter floats or sinks?

What Floats?

Get a coin, a pencil, and other classroom objects. Predict which ones will float. Then fill a large bowl with water. Put each object in the water. Were your predictions right?

Measuring Liquids

You can measure liquids. You can use a measuring cup to find out how much space a liquid takes up. You can use a balance to measure its mass.

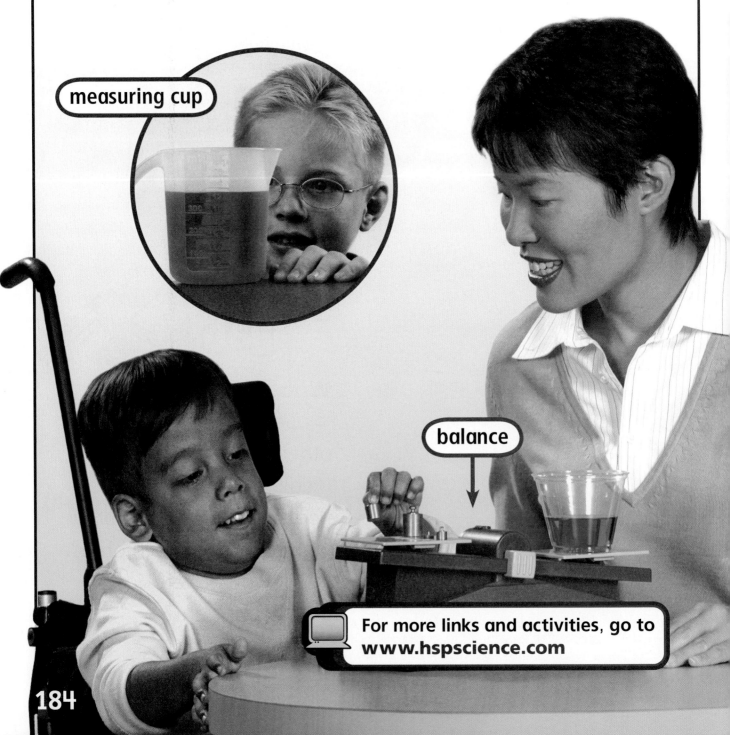

measuring cup

balance

For more links and activities, go to www.hspscience.com

1. MAIN IDEA AND DETAILS Copy and complete this chart.

Liquids

Main Idea
A liquid is matter that **A** _____.
It **B** _____ its own shape.

detail
Some matter dissolves in liquids.

detail
Some matter **C** _____, and some floats.

2. SUMMARIZE Use the chart to write a lesson summary.

3. VOCABULARY Use **sink** and **float** to talk about this picture.

Test Prep

4. Which tool would you use to measure the mass of a liquid?

   A. a balance

   B. a hand lens

   C. a pen

   D. a ruler

Links

Health

Healthful Liquids

Draw pictures of liquids people can drink. Sort them into two groups—good for you and not good for you. Talk about why you sorted them as you did.

 For more links and activities, go to www.hspscience.com

185

Cleaning Up Oil

Oil spills can happen when a boat carrying oil hits something. Oil is one liquid that does not mix with water. It floats on water.

Oil pollutes water in oceans, lakes, or rivers. It also hurts animals. Scientists worked to find ways to clean up oil spills.

When oil spills into the ocean, it is very hard to clean up. Workers must use special soap and sponges to clean up the oil.

THINK ABOUT IT

How can oil spills harm the environment?

Well Oiled

Oil is a heavy, sticky liquid. Some of it is even used to heat houses.

Find out more! Log on to
www.hspscience.com

Making **Protective** Packages

Have you ever opened a milk carton and a bad smell came out? That is because the milk turned sour. Milk turns sour after about 14 days.

A scientist named Manuel Marquez Sanchez has made a new kind of milk carton. This new carton changes color. It changes color when the milk inside it is turning sour. Sanchez is also trying to make other food packages better.

188

You Can Do It!

Materials
- water
- 2 ice cube trays
- freezer

Explore Cooling

What to Do

1. Fill both trays with water.
2. Put one tray in a freezer. Put the other on a table.
3. Wait a few hours. Then look at each tray. What happened?

Draw Conclusions
How did the liquid water change in the freezer? Why?

Mixtures All Around

Many things are mixtures. Choose a mixture in your classroom. Draw it. Then look for the different kinds of matter that are in it. Label each kind. Compare your drawing with a classmate's.

Review and Test Preparation

Vocabulary Review

Tell which picture goes best with each word.

1. solid p. 173   **3. liquid** p. 180

2. mass p. 176   **4. float** p. 182

A.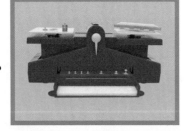

C.

B.

D.

Check Understanding

5. Tell why this is a mixture.

6. Which is a liquid?

    A. air

    B. clay

    C. milk

    D. paper

Critical Thinking

7. How can you **compare** these

(Focus Skill) objects?

8. Think of a solid object. How could you measure it? Write a plan.

Vocabulary

motion

speed

force

push

pull

I wonder...

What makes a roller coaster move?

What do you wonder?

193

How Do Things Move?

The Blue Angels jets move very fast. They also move in many directions as they do tricks. You can classify objects by the ways they move.

Ways Objects Move

You need

• objects

Step 1

Move each object.
Observe the way
it moves.

Step 2

Classify the objects by
the ways they move.
Then write about the
groups you made.

Step 3

Talk with classmates
about your groups.
Compare your results.

Inquiry Skill

Classify the objects by
grouping those that move
the same way.

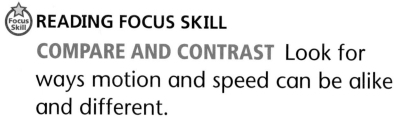

READING FOCUS SKILL

COMPARE AND CONTRAST Look for ways motion and speed can be alike and different.

Motion

Things are in motion all around you. When something is in **motion**, it is moving. What is moving here?

jump rope

race car

Objects move at different speeds. **Speed** is how fast something moves. Both of these objects are moving. They are not moving at the same speed. Which is moving faster?

★ Focus Skill **COMPARE AND CONTRAST** How can speeds of objects be different?

tricycle

How Objects Move

	0	1	2	3	4	5	6	7
straight line								
curve								
circle								
zigzag								

Insta-Lab

Motion Graph

Test some toys. Do they move in a straight path, a curved path, a circle, or a zigzag? Record. Then make a bar graph to show how many toys move in each way.

How Things Move

Things may move in different ways. An object may move in a straight path. It may move in a curved path. It may go in a circle. It may even move in a zigzag.

zigzag

curved path

circle

straight path

For more links and activities, go to
www.hspscience.com

Focus Skill

1. COMPARE AND CONTRAST Copy and complete this chart.

Motion

alike

All objects in **A** _____ are moving.

different

The **B** _____ of an object can be fast or slow.

An object may move in a straight path, in a curved path, in a circle, or in a **C** _____.

2. SUMMARIZE Use the chart to write a summary of this lesson.

3. VOCABULARY Tell about the **motion** in this picture.

Test Prep

4. What are some different ways objects can move?

Links

 Writing

Write About Motion
Think of a sport or an active game you like to play. How do you move your body? Write a description. Tell how your body moves when you play.

I play soccer. I run in a zigzag.

For more links and activities, go to **www.hspscience.com**

199

2

How Can You Change the Way Things Move?

Fast Fact

This man is a juggler. He can juggle 3 pins at a time. You can plan an investigation to find out ways to make objects move.

Pulling and Pushing Objects

You need

● small cube ● objects to make cube move

Step 1

Look at the objects.
How can you use them
to push or pull the cube?
Plan an investigation.

Step 2

Follow your **plan**.
Tell how you moved the
cube. Use the words
push and **pull**.

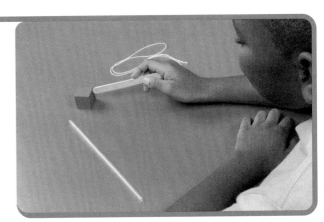

Step 3

Repeat your **plan**.
Do you get the same
results?

Inquiry Skill

You can **plan an
investigation.** Think of
ways to move the cube,
and then try them.

VOCABULARY
force
push
pull

 READING FOCUS SKILL

CAUSE AND EFFECT Look for actions that cause objects to move.

Making Things Move

A **force** makes something move or stop moving. You use force each time you move an object. You use force to move your body, too.

Pushes and pulls are forces. When you **push** an object, you move it away from you. When you **pull** an object, you move it closer to you.

⭐ **CAUSE AND EFFECT** What happens when you push an object?

pulling

pushing

203

Changing Speed

You use force to change the speed of an object. These balls are moving very fast. You can push to stop a ball. Then you can pull it close. You can also push it away by kicking to make it move faster.

⭐ **Focus Skill** **CAUSE AND EFFECT** What may cause a ball to move faster?

pushing away

pulling toward

204

Changing Direction

You use force to change an object's direction. When you play baseball, the ball moves toward you. Then you hit it with the bat. Hitting the ball is a push. The ball moves away from you.

⭐ **CAUSE AND EFFECT** What happens to a ball when you hit it?

Insta-Lab

Push and Pull a Ball

Play ball with classmates. Throw and kick a ball to one another. Each time you touch the ball, tell whether you use a push or a pull.

What force does the boy use to change the ball's direction?

205

Changing Position

You use force to change where an object is. You can pull part of a toy truck up and push part of it down. You can push a toy truck inside the station and pull it outside. You can push it forward and pull it backward.

CAUSE AND EFFECT How can you change where an object is?

up and down

inside and outside

forward and backward

206

1. CAUSE AND EFFECT Copy and complete this chart.

Force

cause   effects

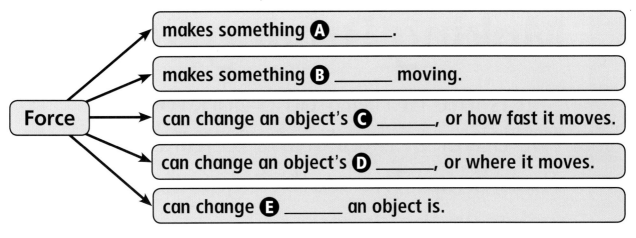

Force

- makes something **A** _____.
- makes something **B** _____ moving.
- can change an object's **C** _____, or how fast it moves.
- can change an object's **D** _____, or where it moves.
- can change **E** _____ an object is.

2. DRAW CONCLUSIONS What force do you use when you jump?

3. VOCABULARY Use the word **push** to tell about the picture.

Test Prep

4. Write a sentence about what causes objects to move or stop moving.

Links

 Math

Adding to Keep Score

In some games, players push objects to score points. Make your own pushing game. Use a box lid. Push a bottle cap from one end to score points. Do this 3 times. Add your points to find your score.

 For more links and activities, go to www.hspscience.com

Making Driving Safer

It is late at night on a dark road. The driver of a car starts to fall asleep. Then, snap! The seatbelt gets tight. It wakes up the driver!

In the past, people did not worry about falling asleep. They used wagons and horses to get places. Then cars took the place of the wagons. These cars were slow. The cars got faster over time.

Driving on roads these days is not very safe. Drivers need to be more careful than ever. This seatbelt is one new tool that keeps drivers safe.

THINK ABOUT IT

Why would a car that goes faster be less safe?

Find out more! Log on to
www.hspscience.com

Moving with Magnets

John Fowler is learning about magnets. He learned that a magnet can pick up things that have iron in them.

John took a magnet off the refrigerator at home. He used it to try to pick up things around the house.

John picked up paper clips. He dropped one in a glass. The magnet even pulled the paper clip through glass and water!

210

You Can Do It!

Make a Magnetic Toy

What to Do

1. Cut a small kite from tissue paper.

2. Tie a paper clip to a thread. Tape the clip to the kite. Tape the end of the thread to a table.

3. Hold the magnet above the kite but without touching the kite. Can you use the magnet to make your kite fly?

Materials

- scissors
- thread
- tissue paper
- paper clip
- tape
- magnet

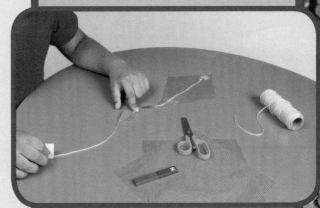

Draw Conclusions

What part of the kite does the magnet pull? Why?

Wheel Hunt

How are a bicycle, a car, and a truck alike? They have wheels. Wheels help objects move. Look around for objects with wheels. Tell how each one moves.

Wheels

truck

car

Review and Test Preparation

Vocabulary Review

Choose the word that best completes each sentence.

motion p. 196   **force** p. 202

speed p. 197   **pull** p. 203

1. A ___ makes something move.

2. When something is moving, it is in ___ .

3. How fast an object moves is its ___ .

4. A ___ is a force that moves an object closer to you.

Check Understanding

5. Use these pictures to **compare** different
(Focus Skill) ways objects can move.

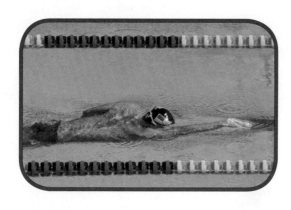

6. Look at this picture. What is **causing** the stroller to move?

A. speed

B. pushing

C. motion

D. pulling

Critical Thinking

7. How can you change the speed of a ball?

8. List these objects in order from slowest to fastest.

A.

B.

C.

World's Tallest Fountain

Fountain Hills

You may not believe your eyes!

In Fountain Hills, Arizona, there is a very tall water fountain. It is so tall, you can see it from any place in town.

People say it's the world's tallest water fountain. And it sits in the middle of a lake.

Why Is It So Big?

The fountain has three powerful pumps. The pumps push the water into the air for 15 minutes each hour. Pushing the water is hard work!

When all three pumps push the water, it goes high into the sky. It rises higher than the Washington Monument in Washington, D.C.

A set of powerful pumps

The fountain rises higher than the Washington Monument.

Think and Do

1. SCIENCE AND TECHNOLOGY Builders used technology to help them make the water from the fountain go high into the air. Imagine that you were asked to make a fountain. What technology or instruments would you use to help build it? How will these instruments help you make the fountain send water high into the air? Draw a picture of your fountain. Use words and sentences to describe its design.

2. SCIENTIFIC THINKING Look carefully at the picture of the fountain. What materials were used to build it? List what you think might have been used and why.

Deer Valley Rock Art Center

Phoenix

Do you like to look at pictures? If you do, visit the Deer Valley Rock Art Center.

The center is in Phoenix. Many years ago, Native Americans lived here. They carved or painted pictures on rocks.

Learn about the past at this park.

rock art center

Special Pictures

Rock art designs were made on the surfaces of rock. Petroglyphs are one kind of rock art.

There are over 1,500 petroglyphs in the park.

Native Americans made rock art for different reasons. They may have made the rock art to tell a story. Or they wanted to record an event.

Think and Do

1. SCIENCE AND TECHNOLOGY Petroglyphs are made by carving or tapping through the rock's top layer. What tools do you think Native Americans used to make petroglyphs? Write down your ideas.

2. SCIENTIFIC THINKING Imagine that you are a Native American of long ago. You want to tell a story about your pet. Tell the story just by drawing pictures. What drawings will you use to tell your story?

All Aboard!

Gila River
Indian Community

How would you like to go for a ride in a stagecoach?

Well, at Rawhide Western Town, you can.

When you visit an old western town you can see how people lived many years ago.

You can also have fun on the stagecoach.

Let's go for a ride!

A Way to Travel

Long ago, people used stagecoaches to go from town to town. Stagecoaches could go where railroads couldn't.

The stagecoaches had wooden tops and wooden wheels. Horses pulled them.

Stagecoaches helped move mail and newspapers. They also moved gold and money all over the country.

Think and Do

1. SCIENCE AND TECHNOLOGY Stagecoaches had wheels that were made out of wood. What materials are wheels made out of today? Would it have been hard to travel on wooden wheels? Why? Make a chart of the different vehicles that use wheels today. How are the wheels the same? How are they different?

2. SCIENTIFIC THINKING Imagine you are going to be driving a stagecoach. Write and draw pictures describing all of the things you would need to learn how to do, as well as what happened on your trip.

Heat Changes Food

Materials
- lamp
- aluminum foil
- a cracker, an ice cube, chocolate chips, butter

What to Do
1. Place a cracker, an ice cube, some chocolate chips, and some butter on separate pieces of foil.
2. Put them under a hot lamp.
3. Check them every five minutes.
4. Make a chart to show what happened.

Draw Conclusions
1. What happened to the cracker?
2. What happened to the other food?

How Will a Ball Move?

Materials
- tape
- ball
- ramp
- books

What to Do
1. Think about how a ball moves. Set up the ramp.
2. Predict where the ball will stop when you roll it down the ramp. Mark the spot with tape.
3. Let the ball roll down the ramp. Do not push it.
4. Was your prediction correct? Explain what you found out.

Draw Conclusions
1. Did thinking about how a ball moves help your prediction?
2. How can you make the ball move differently?

UNIT C

Earth and Space Science

TO: lashonda@hspscience.com

FROM: marcus@hspscience2.com

RE: Meteor Crater

Dear Lashonda,

I just got back from my science field trip. We went to Meteor Crater, near Winslow. Thousands of years ago, a big rock from space hit Earth. It made a bowl-shaped area called a crater. It would take an hour to walk all the way around the crater! You should go see it.

Your pal,

Marcus

Experiment!

Starry, Starry Night As you do this unit, you will learn about things you can see in the sky. How is the nighttime sky different from the daytime sky? Plan and do a test to find out.

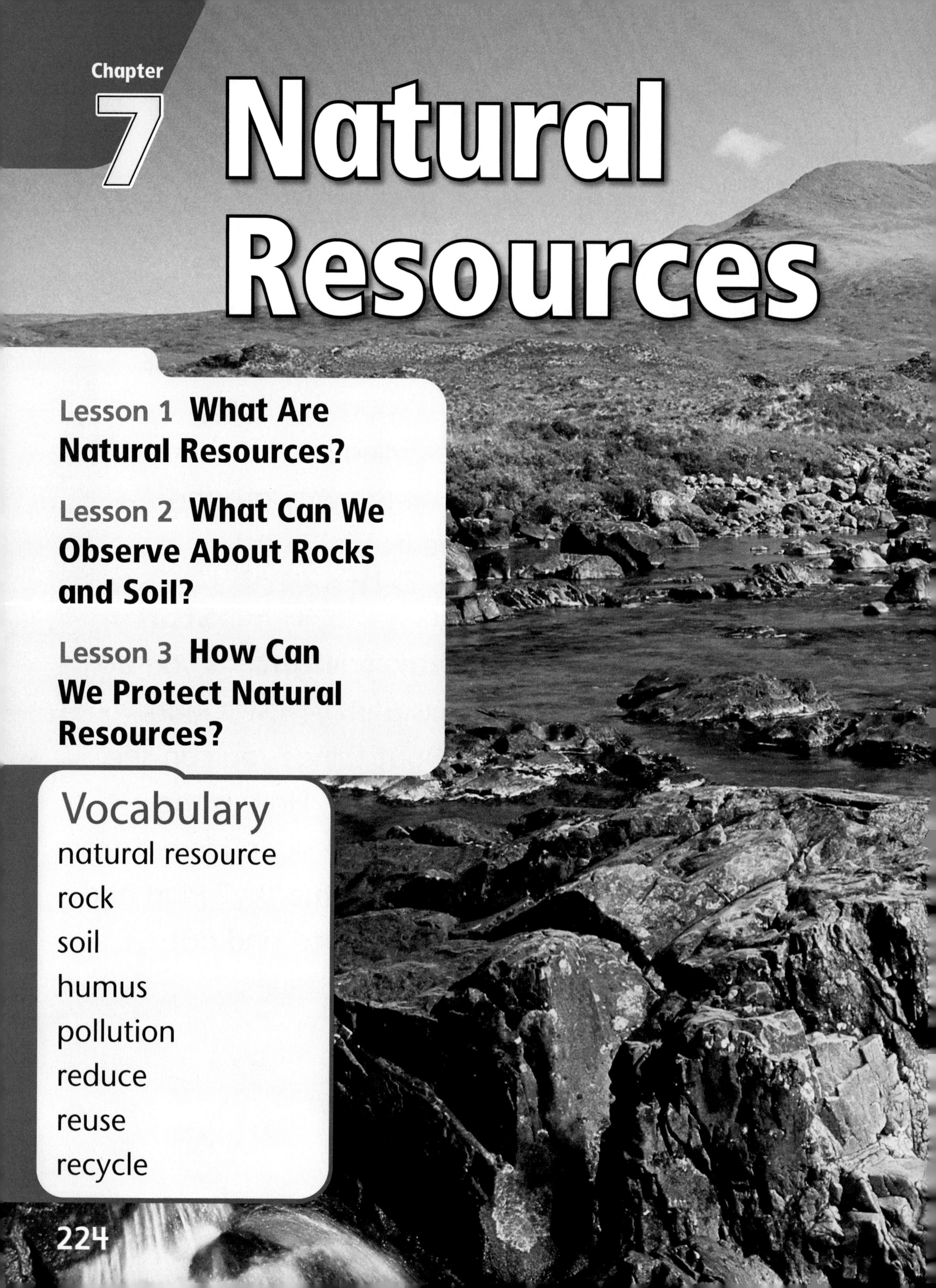

Chapter 7

Natural Resources

Lesson 1 What Are Natural Resources?

Lesson 2 What Can We Observe About Rocks and Soil?

Lesson 3 How Can We Protect Natural Resources?

Vocabulary

natural resource
rock
soil
humus
pollution
reduce
reuse
recycle

I wonder...

Where does water come from?

What do you wonder?

225

What Are Natural Resources?

Fast Fact

Long ago, people used moving air, or wind, to travel in sailing ships. You can observe ways people use natural resources.

All Around You

You need

● crayons

● construction paper

Step 1

Make a chart like this one.

Things I Saw Outdoors	
animals	plants
water	land

Step 2

Go outside. **Observe** everything around you. Draw and label the things that belong in the chart.

Step 3

Share your chart with a classmate. Did you both **observe** the same things?

Inquiry Skill

When you **observe**, you use your senses to find out about things.

227

READING FOCUS SKILL

MAIN IDEA AND DETAILS Look for the main ideas about natural resources.

Natural Resources

A **natural resource** is anything from nature that people can use. Water and air are natural resources. Rocks and soil are natural resources. Plants and animals are natural resources that live on land, in water, and in air.

MAIN IDEA AND DETAILS
What is a natural resource?

> What natural resources do you see in this picture?

How are these people using water?

Water

Water is a natural resource that all living things need. People drink water and use it to clean and to cook. People travel on water, too.

 MAIN IDEA AND DETAILS
What are some ways people use water?

Can Water Cool You?

Wrap one thermometer in a damp towel. Wrap another in a dry towel. Check them after 10 minutes. Which is cooler? How can you use water to keep your body cool?

229

Air

Air is a natural resource. You can not see air, but it is all around you. Many living things need air to live. People and many animals breathe air. People use air to fill things such as balloons. They also use air to make things move.

Focus Skill **MAIN IDEA AND DETAILS** What are some ways people use air?

How are these people using air?

1. MAIN IDEA AND DETAILS Copy and complete this chart.

> **Main Idea**
> A **A** _____ is anything from nature that people can use.

> **detail**
> People use **B** _____ for drinking, cleaning, and cooking.

> **detail**
> People and many animals breathe **C** _____.

> **detail**
> Plants, animals, rocks, and soil are some other natural resources.

2. DRAW CONCLUSIONS Is everything that people use a natural resource? Explain.

3. VOCABULARY Use the words **natural resource** to talk about this picture.

Test Prep

4. How do people use air?
- **A.** They drink it.
- **B.** They build with it.
- **C.** They clean with it.
- **D.** They breathe it.

Links

Writing

Water Poem
Make a list of sounds that water can make. Use your list to write a poem about water. Draw a picture.

 For more links and activities, go to www.hspscience.com

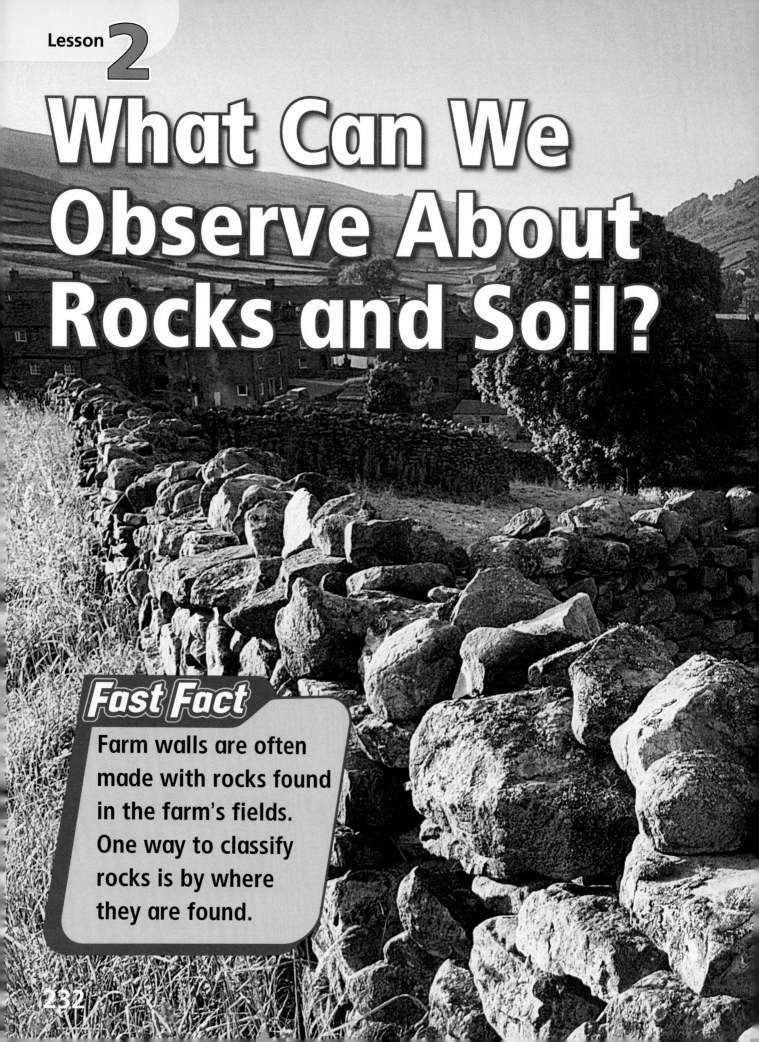

What Can We Observe About Rocks and Soil?

Fast Fact

Farm walls are often made with rocks found in the farm's fields. One way to classify rocks is by where they are found.

Classify Rocks

You need

- hand lens
- rocks

Step 1

Use a hand lens to observe each rock.

Step 2

Sort the rocks by grouping those that are the same. Make a chart to show how you **classified** the rocks.

Rocks			
White			

Step 3

Use the chart to tell how the rocks are alike. Then tell how they are different.

Inquiry Skill

You **classify** things by the ways they are alike.

VOCABULARY
rock
soil
humus

 **READING FOCUS SKILL**

COMPARE AND CONTRAST Look for ways rocks and kinds of soil are alike. Also look for ways they are different.

Rocks

A **rock** is a hard, nonliving thing that comes from Earth. Rocks are a natural resource.

The walls of this building are made of rock.

234

People use rocks in different ways. They build with rocks. They carve some rocks into statues. Some things from rocks, such as salt, are in the food you eat.

★ **COMPARE AND CONTRAST**
Compare some ways people use rocks.

Pretzels have salt on them. People get salt from rocks.

This statue is made of a kind of rock called marble.

235

Soil

The top layer of Earth is **soil**. Soil is made up of clay, sand, and humus. Clay and sand are small pieces of rock. **Humus** is pieces of dead plants and animals. Soil in different places may have different amounts of sand, humus, and clay.

sand

+

humus

+

clay

=

soil

236

Soil is a natural resource. Some kinds can hold more water than other kinds. People use soil to grow plants for food. Plants take water and other things they need from soil.

A girl plants seeds in soil.

⭐ **COMPARE AND CONTRAST**
How are kinds of soil alike and different?

Insta-Lab

Hold It!

Put a coffee filter on a cup. Hold it in place with a rubber band. Put soil on the filter. Pour $\frac{1}{2}$ cup of water onto the soil. Measure the water that passes through into the cup. How much water did the soil hold?

Other Things in Soil

Different things may be in soil. Worms and other animals may live there. Plant roots grow down into soil. Pieces of dead plants and animals may be in soil. Small rocks may be in it, too.

Focus Skill **COMPARE AND CONTRAST** Compare some of the different things found in soil.

dead plant

roots

worm

rock

Focus Skill

1. COMPARE AND CONTRAST Copy and complete this chart.

> **Rocks and Soil**

alike	different
All are hard, nonliving things that come from **Ⓐ** _____.	People use rocks to build, to carve into **Ⓑ** _____, and to use in food.
Soil is made up of sand, **Ⓒ** _____, and clay.	Different things, such as roots and rocks, may be in soil.

2. SUMMARIZE Use the chart to write a summary of the lesson.

3. VOCABULARY Use the words **rock** and **soil** to tell about this picture.

Test Prep

4. Why are rocks and soil natural resources?

Links

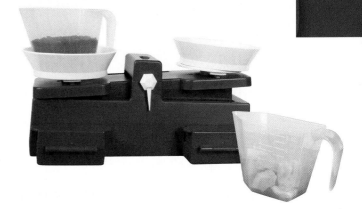

Math 123

Compare Rock and Soil Masses
Get $\frac{1}{2}$ cup of soil and $\frac{1}{2}$ cup of small rocks. Use a balance to compare their masses. Then draw pictures and write >, <, or = to show what you found out.

 For more links and activities, go to www.hspscience.com

How Can We Protect Natural Resources?

Fast Fact

Some of the things on playgrounds are made from recycled plastic jugs! You can draw a conclusion about why people should recycle things.

240

What Happens to Trash?

You need

 • lettuce    • napkin   • piece of foam cup    • pan of soil

Step 1

Bury the lettuce, the napkin, and the piece of foam cup in the soil.

Step 2

Water the soil every three days. After two weeks, dig up the things. What do you **observe**?

Step 3

Draw a conclusion. How could trash harm the land? Why?

Inquiry Skill

Use what you observe and what you know to **draw a conclusion.**

241

VOCABULARY

pollution
reduce
reuse
recycle

 READING FOCUS SKILL

CAUSE AND EFFECT Look for ways people can take care of natural resources.

Taking Care of Resources

Pollution harms our natural resources. **Pollution** is waste that causes harm to land, water, and air. Pollution also causes harm to plants and animals.

People can pick up trash on land.

242

People can help take care of natural resources. They can put trash in its place. They can clean up trash. They can also walk or ride bikes instead of using cars. Cars and trucks make air pollution and use natural resources.

CAUSE AND EFFECT What does pollution cause?

People can walk instead of using cars.

People can pick up trash in water.

Reduce, Reuse, Recycle

People can help care for natural resources. They can reduce, reuse, and recycle. This makes less trash. It also helps save natural resources.

To **reduce** something means to use less of it. People can use cloth bags. This reduces the number of paper and plastic bags that are used.

To **reuse** means to use something again. People can reuse food jars. The jars can hold pencils and other things.

To **recycle** means to use old things to make new things. People can recycle newpapers. The old papers can be made into new paper.

⭐ Focus Skill **CAUSE AND EFFECT** What effect does recycling have on the amount of trash?

Insta-Lab

Reuse an Egg Carton

Decorate an egg carton. Use it to store things you collect. You can keep different kinds of things in the different cups.

245

Ways to Save Resources

This family is saving resources.

How is each family member helping?

Turn off the lights when you leave a room.

Turn off the water when you do not need it.

Turn down the heat. Put on a sweater to stay warm.

Recycle.

For more links and activities, go to
www.hspscience.com

1. CAUSE AND EFFECT Copy and complete this chart.

Natural Resources

cause		effect
People make pollution.	→	Pollution harms our **A** _____.
People clean up **B** _____.	→	People take care of resources.
People **C** _____, reuse, and recycle.	→	People make less **D** _____.

2. DRAW CONCLUSIONS
How can you take care of resources at your home?

3. VOCABULARY Use the word **pollution** to talk about this picture.

Test Prep
4. How do reducing, reusing, and recycling help?
  A. They make pollution.
  B. They harm land, water, and air.
  C. They help save natural resources.
  D. They harm plants and animals.

Links

Math 1₂3

Counting by Fours
Every person makes about 4 pounds of trash each day. How much trash would you make in 2 days, in 5 days, and in 1 week? Use a number line or counters to help you count by fours. Show your work in a chart.

How Much Trash?	
days	pounds of trash
1	4
2	8
5	
7	

For more links and activities, go to
www.hspscience.com

Be Earth's Friend

Earth Day is a time for people to think about taking care of Earth. People can keep plants and animals healthy. They can also help keep Earth clean.

1. Reduce.

Each person in the United States makes about 2 kilograms (4 pounds) of trash every day! So landfills, or places where people dump trash, are starting to get full.

People should reduce the amount of trash they throw away.

2. Reuse.

Some trash in landfills could be used for other things! People should find more ways to reuse trash.

3. Recycle.

Paper takes up the largest amount of space in most landfills. Paper can be easily recycled.

People can recycle by taking old newspapers to a recycling center.

4. Respect.

Many times people forget to respect, or care for, Earth. One way to show respect for Earth is to use fewer resources.

Respect Earth by turning off the water while you brush your teeth.

THINK ABOUT IT

What does Earth Day teach people about natural resources?

Find out more! Log on to
www.hspscience.com

249

Studying Rivers

Dr. Ruth Patrick is a nature scientist. Her father taught her to love plants, streams, and rivers.

Dr. Patrick looks at how pollution can hurt a river. Dr. Patrick studies the plants and animals that live in rivers. She makes a list of things scientists can check to see if a river is polluted. Dr. Patrick helps keep our rivers clean.

Making Water Clean

What to Do

1. Mix salt in water. Taste it. Pour it into the tub of sand.

2. Put the other cup inside the tub. Cover the tub. Use the rubber band to hold the plastic in place. Put marbles on top.

3. Put the tub in the sun for two hours. Then take out the cup. Taste the water.

Materials

- salt
- 2 cups
- water
- spoon
- tub of sand
- plastic wrap
- rubber band
- 3 marbles

Draw Conclusions

What do you think happened to the water?

Too Much Packaging

Some foods come in packages that make lots of trash. Look at foods in your kitchen. Draw those that have too much packaging. Then draw to show how these foods could have less packaging.

Juice boxes have too much packaging. You could buy jars of juice.

251

Review and Test Preparation

Vocabulary Review

Tell which picture goes best with each word or words.

1. natural resource

p. 228

A.

2. rock p. 234

B.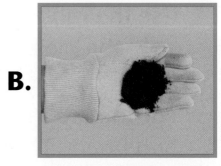

3. humus p. 236

C.

4. recycle p. 245

D.

Check Understanding

5. Tell the **details** about the natural resources in this picture.

(Focus Skill)

6. Which part of soil is pieces of dead plants and animals?

A. clay

B. humus

C. rock

D. soil

7. Which of these harms natural resources?

F. air   **H.** pollution

G. humus   **J.** recycling

Critical Thinking

8. You want to take care of resources in your school. Write a plan. Tell each thing you would do. Tell why each thing would help.

Chapter 8

Objects in the Sky

Vocabulary

sun

star

moon

rotate

crater

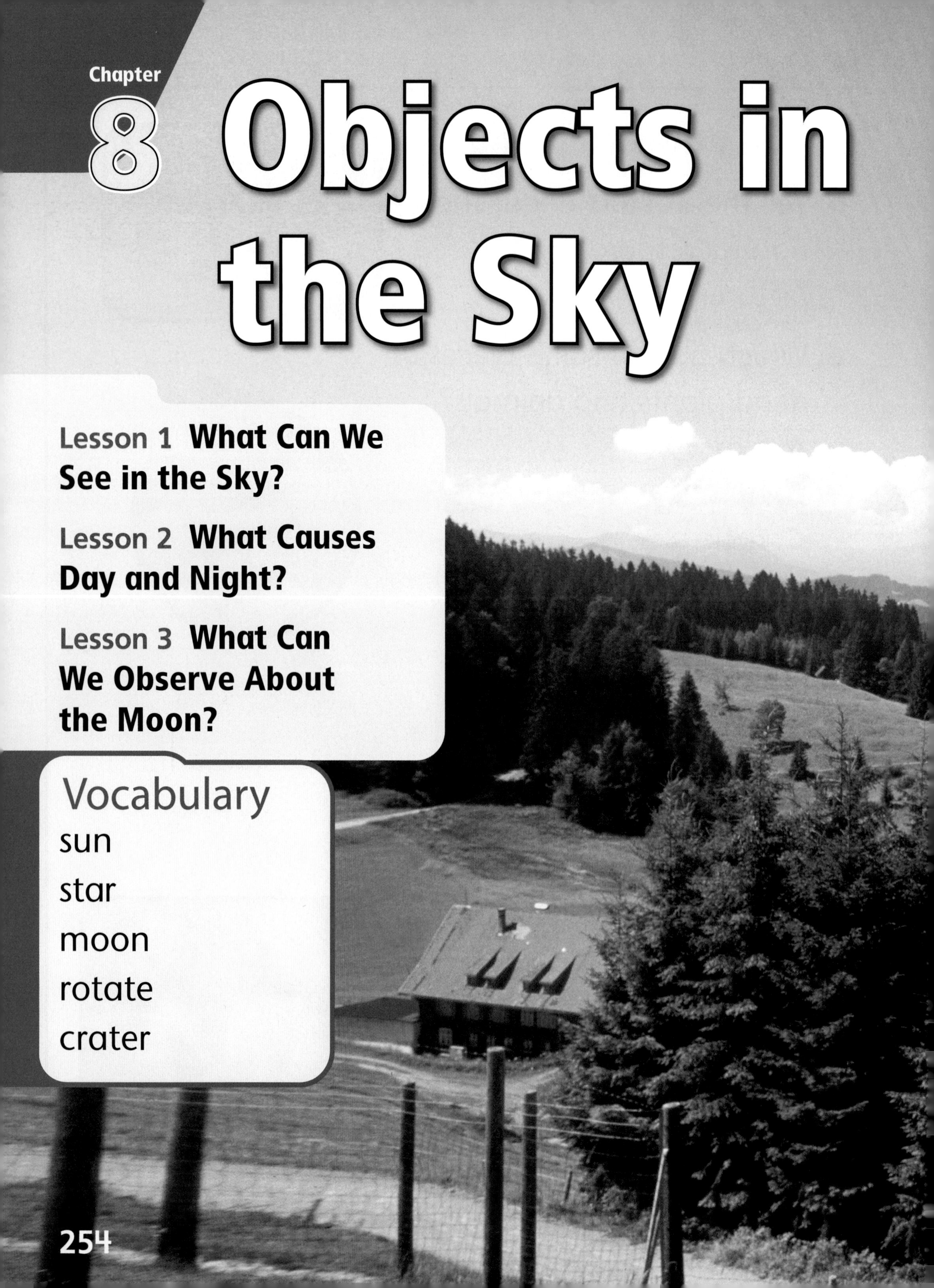

I wonder...

Why can you sometimes see the moon in the daytime?

What do **you** wonder?

What Can We See in the Sky?

Fast Fact

Moving air causes some of the light from the stars to bend. This makes the stars seem to twinkle. You can communicate about what you see in the sky.

The Daytime Sky

You need

• **colored paper**　　• **crayons**

Look out the window.
Observe the daytime sky.

Draw pictures of what
you see. Write about it.

Share your work with a
partner. Use it to help
you **communicate** what
you observed.

Inquiry Skill

You can use writing and
pictures to help you
communicate.

VOCABULARY
sun
star
moon

 READING FOCUS SKILL

COMPARE AND CONTRAST Look for ways the daytime and nighttime skies are alike and ways they are different.

Observing the Sky

In the daytime sky, you may see clouds and the sun. The **sun** is the star closest to Earth. A **star** is an object in the sky that gives off its own light. The sun lights Earth in the daytime.

sun

clouds

In the nighttime sky, you may see stars, planets, and the moon. The **moon** is a huge ball of rock. It does not give off its own light. Its light comes from the sun.

moon

⭐ **COMPARE AND CONTRAST** How are the daytime sky and the nighttime sky different?

planet

stars

Insta-Lab

Moonlight

Cover a ball with foil. Have a partner shine a flashlight at the ball. Does the ball seem brighter when it is lit up? How is the ball like the moon? How is the flashlight like the sun?

Telescopes

You can look at the sky with a telescope. A telescope is a tool that makes things that are far away look closer. It can help you see more of the moon, stars, and planets.

Look at the planet Mars with just your eyes. This is what you see.

Look at Mars with a telescope. This is what you see. How much more can you see now?

For more links and activities, go to www.hspscience.com

1. COMPARE AND CONTRAST Copy and complete this chart.

alike

> In the daytime sky and nighttime sky, you can sometimes see clouds and the moon.

different

> In the daytime sky, you may see **Ⓐ** _____ and the sun.

> In the nighttime sky, you may see **Ⓑ** _____, planets, and the moon.

> In the daytime, the **Ⓒ** _____ gives off light.

> In the nighttime, the stars give off light, but the **Ⓓ** _____ does not.

2. DRAW CONCLUSIONS Why do you think the sun is much brighter than the moon?

3. VOCABULARY Use the words **sun** and **star** to talk about this picture.

Test Prep

4. What does a telescope do?
  A. It makes things that are far away look closer.
  B. It makes things that are close look farther away.
  C. It makes very big things look farther away.
  D. It makes very big things look smaller.

Links

Writing

Stories About the Sky

Long ago, people made up stories about what they saw in the sky. Write your own story about something in the sky. Then draw a picture for your story.

The sun is a happy teacher. The clouds are her students.

For more links and activities, go to www.hspscience.com

What Causes Day and Night?

Fast Fact

When it is daytime in the United States, it is nighttime in China. You can make a model to see why this happens.

Model Day and Night

You need

- **labels**
- **tape**
- **globe**
- **flashlight**

Step 1

Label the globe **Earth**.
Label the flashlight **sun**.
Use them to **make a model**
of Earth and the sun.

Step 2

Make the room dark. Have
a partner hold the globe.
Shine the flashlight on it.

Step 3

How does the **model**
help you see why Earth
has day and night?

Inquiry Skill

Make a model to help
you see why something
happens.

VOCABULARY
rotate

READING FOCUS SKILL

CAUSE AND EFFECT Look for what causes day and night.

Day and Night

Each day, the sun seems to move across the sky. It is not the sun that is moving. It is Earth! Earth rotates. To **rotate** is to spin like a top.

United States

day

As Earth rotates, the side we live on turns toward the sun. The sun lights the sky, and we have day. As Earth keeps rotating, our side turns away from the sun. The sky gets dark, and we have night.

CAUSE AND EFFECT **What do we have when the side of Earth we live on turns toward the sun? Why?**

United States

night

Objects in the Sky Seem to Move

The sun, moon, and stars seem to move in the sky. As Earth spins, we turn toward and away from the sun, moon, and stars. We can not feel that we are moving, so it seems to us as if they are.

Things Seem to Move

Stand in an open space. Turn around in circles. Do the things around you seem to move? How is this like the way the sun and stars seem to move around Earth?

CAUSE AND EFFECT Why does the sun seem to move in the sky?

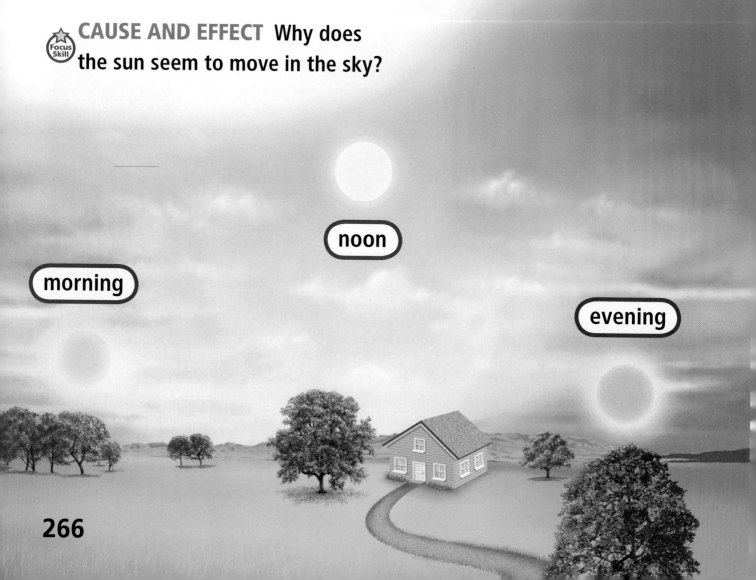

noon

morning

evening

1. CAUSE AND EFFECT Copy and complete this chart.

> **Day and Night**

cause

As Earth **Ⓐ** _____, the side we live on turns toward the sun.

The side we live on turns away from the **Ⓓ** _____.

effect

The **Ⓑ** _____ lights the sky, and we have **Ⓒ** _____.

We have **Ⓔ** _____.

2. SUMMARIZE Use the chart to write a summary of the lesson.

3. VOCABULARY Use the word **rotate** to talk about this picture.

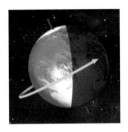

Test Prep

4. Why do we have daytime when China has nighttime?

Math

Time and the Sun

Observe the sun at 8:00 A.M., noon, and 7:00 P.M. Draw and write about what you observe. Then make a prediction. Will the sun be in about the same places at the same times tomorrow? Tell why. Check tomorrow to see if you were right.

8 A.M.
The sun is behind Mrs. King's house.

 For more links and activities, go to www.hspscience.com

What Can We Observe About the Moon?

Fast Fact

Much of the moon is covered with dust. It has many craters. You can use what you know to infer how the craters were made.

268

The Surface of the Moon

You need

- pan of sand

- spray bottle of water

- marbles

Step 1

Spray the sand lightly with water.

Step 2

Hold the marbles above the sand. Drop them one at a time. Observe.

Step 3

Infer how the moon's craters were made. Compare your ideas with others' ideas.

Inquiry Skill

To infer, first observe. Then think about what you see.

VOCABULARY
crater

 READING FOCUS SKILL

SEQUENCE Look for the order in which the moon seems to change.

Changes in the Moon's Shape

The shape of the moon seems to change a little each night. The changes make a pattern that takes about 29 days.

On some nights, you can not see the moon at all. Then you start to see a little of it. After about 15 days, you see the moon as a full circle. Then you see less of it each night. In about 14 more days, you can not see it again.

Day 22
quarter moon

 SEQUENCE What happens to the moon after you see it as a full circle?

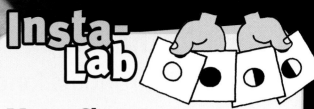

Moon Changes

The picture cards show how the moon looks. Put them in order. Start with the new moon. Then use the pictures to tell about how the moon seems to change.

**Day 1
new moon**

**Day 8
quarter moon**

**Day 15
full moon**

Exploring the Moon

In 1969, astronauts landed on the moon for the first time. First, they saw the moon's gray dust and craters. A **crater** is a hole that is shaped like a bowl in a surface. Next, the astronauts explored the moon. Later, they brought moon rocks back to Earth.

⭐ **Focus Skill** **SEQUENCE** **What did the astronauts do after they landed on the moon?**

astronaut on the moon

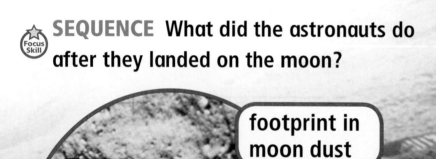

footprint in moon dust

moon rock

Focus Skill

1. SEQUENCE Copy and complete this chart.

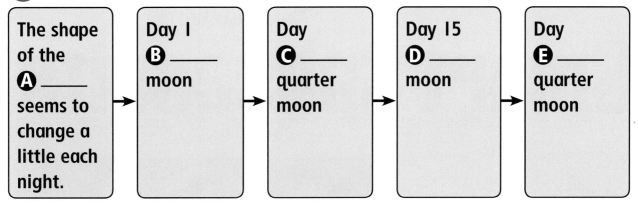

| The shape of the **A** _____ seems to change a little each night. | Day 1 **B** _____ moon | Day **C** _____ quarter moon | Day 15 **D** _____ moon | Day **E** _____ quarter moon |

2. SUMMARIZE Write sentences to summarize this lesson.

3. VOCABULARY Use the word **crater** to talk about this picture.

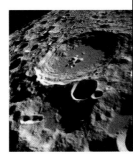

Test Prep

4. How many days is it from one new moon to the next new moon?

A. 8
B. 15
C. 22
D. 29

Links

Writing

Writing About the Moon

Research what the moon is like. Then write sentences about exploring the moon yourself. What would you do there? What would you want to find out? Draw pictures to go with your sentences.

I would walk in the craters.

For more links and activities, go to www.hspscience.com

273

Smart Spacesuits

Right now, people are living and working on the space station. The people are called astronauts.

Spacesuits have to protect astronauts from the cold. The suits also have to let astronauts move their arms and hands. That is so the astronauts can add parts or do repairs.

Breathtaking Fact

When astronauts go outside, they wear special spacesuits. That is because it is very cold in space and there is no air to breathe.

274

Scientists have made the spacesuits better. They added a computer that is sewn into the suit. The computer will help astronauts do their work.

Scientists also made the gloves better. Now, the fingers and thumbs are much easier to move. The gloves are also heated to help the astronauts work outside longer.

THINK ABOUT IT
Why do you think astronauts have to wear special suits?

Find out more! Log on to
www.hspscience.com

Studying Mars

Joy Crisp loves rocks and volcanoes. Now she is studying rocks and volcanoes on Mars. Mars is a planet in space.

Crisp uses machines on Earth to watch two robot rovers on Mars. The rovers are like little radio-controlled trucks. They use special tools to study rocks and dirt.

Scientists are looking to find out if Mars ever had water. If so, scientists say people might someday live on Mars.

Warm or Cool

What to Do

1. When is it warmest outside? Make a chart. Predict what you will find out.

2. Use a thermometer. Find the temperature at three different times of day.

3. Write the temperatures in the chart. Were your predictions correct?

Materials
• thermometer

Draw Conclusions

Why is the temperature different at different times of day? What does the sun do to Earth?

Moon Journal

Keep a moon journal. Go outside with a family member each night for one month. Find the moon. Draw what you observe. Write the date on each picture. After one month, bind your drawings into a book. Share it with the class.

Review and Test Preparation

Vocabulary Review

Choose the best word to complete each sentence.

sun p. 258   **rotate** p. 264

moon p. 259   **crater** p. 272

1. A word that means spin is ___.

2. A ball of rock whose light comes from the sun is the ___.

3. The star closest to Earth is the ___.

4. A hole in the surface of the moon that is shaped like a bowl is a ___.

Check Understanding

5. Explain the **effect** when our side of Earth turns toward the sun. Use this picture to help you.

6. Which object in the sky gives off its own light?

A. cloud   **C.** moon

B. Earth   **D.** star

7. Each photo is part of a **sequence**. Which one shows the moon eight days after a new moon?

 **F.**

 **H.**

 **G.**

 **J.**

Critical Thinking

8. Juan looks at the sky and sees what this picture shows. Tell what you know about each object he sees.

Lesson 1 What Is Weather?

Lesson 2 What Makes Clouds and Rain?

Lesson 3 What Are the Seasons?

Vocabulary

weather	condense
temperature	season
thermometer	spring
water cycle	summer
evaporate	fall
water vapor	winter

I wonder...

What makes a rainbow?

What do **YOU** wonder?

What Is Weather?

Fast Fact

About 25 centimeters (10 inches) of snow equals about 3 centimeters (1 inch) of rain. You can compare snow to other types of weather.

Daily Weather

You need

- paper

- markers

Observe the weather each day for two weeks.

Make a chart. Record what you see.

Daily Weather

Mon.	Tues.	Wed.	Thurs.	Fri.

Compare the weather from day to day. Do you see any patterns? Predict next week's weather.

Inquiry Skill

You can **compare** things by telling how they are alike and how they are different.

Reading in Science

 READING FOCUS SKILL

COMPARE AND CONTRAST Look for ways in which weather can be different from day to day.

Weather

Weather is what the air outside is like. You can see and feel the weather. It may be warm or cool. It may be snowy, windy, rainy, cloudy, or sunny.

What weather do you see here?

Weather can change. It may be sunny one day. The next day may be cloudy. It may be cold for many days. Then it may warm up. One day may be windy. Another day may be calm.

Focus Skill

How can weather be different from day to day?

Insta-Lab

Observing Weather

Look out the window. Observe the sky. Observe what people are wearing. What can you tell about the weather? Repeat each day for a week. Make a chart to show weather data.

Weather and You

You wear heavy clothes in cold weather. You wear light clothes in warm weather. When it rains, you wear clothes that help keep you dry. You may choose activities to go with the weather, too.

Focus Skill **COMPARE AND CONTRAST** How is clothing for cold weather different from clothing for warm weather?

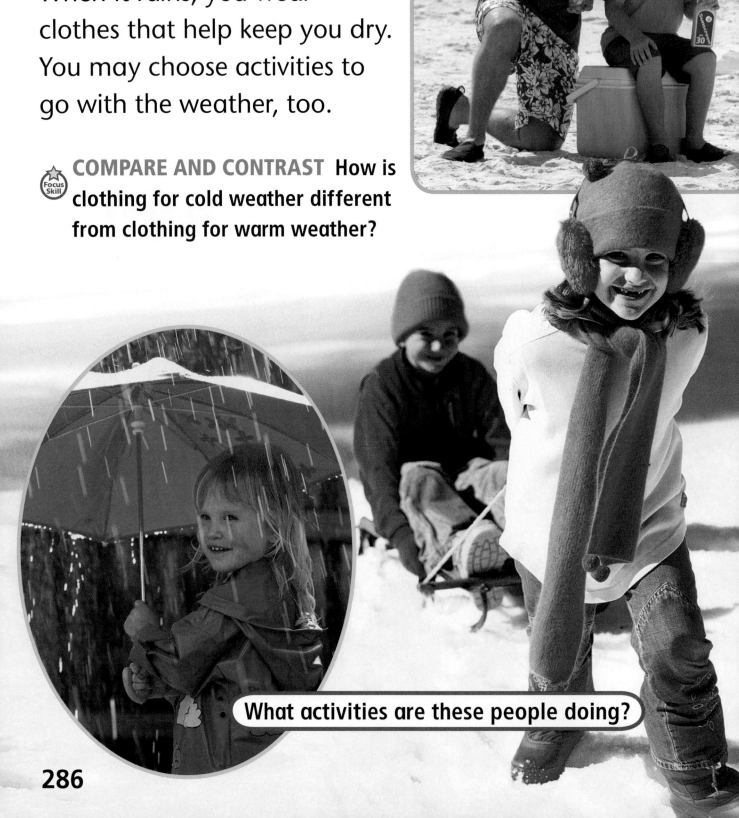

What activities are these people doing?

286

Measuring Temperature and Rain

One way to measure weather is to find the temperature. **Temperature** is the measure of how hot or cold something is. A **thermometer** is a tool for measuring temperature.

You can also measure how much rain falls. A rain gauge shows how much rain has fallen.

thermometer

 COMPARE AND CONTRAST
Focus Skill

How does a thermometer differ from a rain gauge?

rain gauge

287

Measuring Wind

You can measure wind, too. An anemometer measures the speed of the wind. A weather vane shows the direction of the wind. A windsock also shows the direction of the wind.

⭐ **COMPARE AND CONTRAST**
How does an anemometer differ from a windsock?

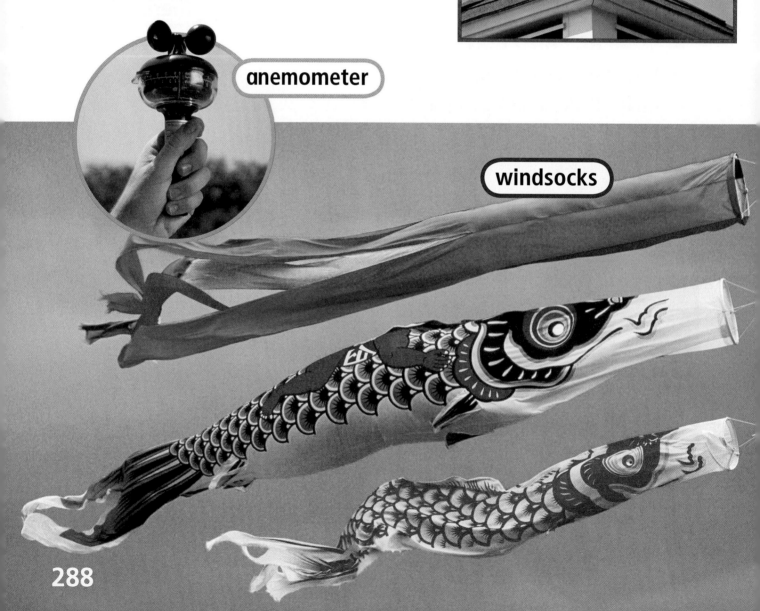

weather vane

anemometer

windsocks

1. COMPARE AND CONTRAST Copy and complete this chart.

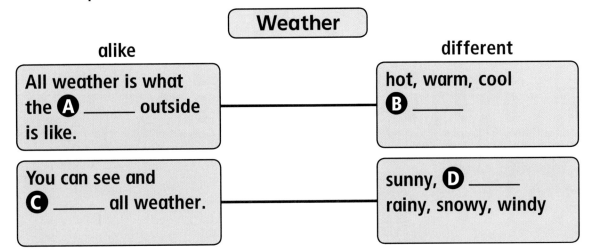

Weather

alike

All weather is what the **A** _____ outside is like.	hot, warm, cool **B** _____
You can see and **C** _____ all weather.	sunny, **D** _____ rainy, snowy, windy

different

2. DRAW CONCLUSIONS
How can measuring weather help people?

3. VOCABULARY
Use the words **temperature** and **thermometer** to tell about the picture.

Test Prep
4. What are three ways you can measure weather?

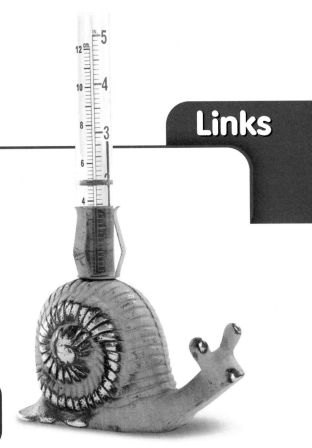

Links

Math

Solve Problems
Juan checked his rain gauge. He saw 5 centimeters of rain on Monday. He saw 3 centimeters more rain on Tuesday. How much rain fell in all?

 For more links and activities, go to www.hspscience.com

289

What Makes Clouds and Rain?

Fast Fact

Rain clouds look dark because they are thick and block the sun. What can you infer about rain and clouds?

290

Make Clouds

You need

 • jar with lid    • hot water    • ice cubes

Step 1

Let your teacher put the hot water in the jar. Wait one minute. Then pour most of it out. **CAUTION:** hot water!

Step 2

Turn the jar lid upside down. Place it on the jar. Observe.

Step 3

Place ice on the lid. Observe. **Infer** how clouds form.

Inquiry Skill

To **infer** what happens, observe carefully. Then draw a conclusion.

Reading in Science

VOCABULARY
water cycle
evaporate
water vapor
condense

READING FOCUS SKILL

CAUSE AND EFFECT Look for what causes clouds and rain to form.

The Water Cycle

Clouds and rain are part of the water cycle. In the **water cycle**, water moves from Earth to the air and back again.

Science Up Close

The Water Cycle

❶ The sun makes water warm. This causes the water to **evaporate**, or change to water vapor. **Water vapor** is water in the air that you can not see.

❷ Water vapor meets cool air. The cool air causes the water vapor to **condense**, or change into tiny water drops. The drops form clouds.

292

3 Water drops come together and get bigger and heavier. Then they fall as rain or snow.

4 Some rain and snow falls into rivers, lakes, and oceans. Some flows there from the land.

5 The cycle continues.

For more links and activities, go to www.hspscience.com

Clouds

Clouds are clues about how the weather may change. Some kind of clouds are shown in the pictures.

⭐ **Focus Skill** **CAUSE AND EFFECT** What kind of cloud brings rain or snow?

Clouds	Weather
 cumulus	Some clouds look like puffy white cotton. They often mean nice weather.
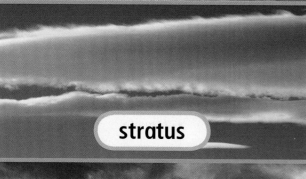 stratus	Other clouds are gray, flat, and low in the sky. They may bring rain or snow.
 cirrus	These clouds look like thin, white feathers. They often mean sunny weather.

294

1. CAUSE AND EFFECT Copy and complete this chart.

The Water Cycle

cause | effect

| Sun heats water. | → | Water Ⓐ _____. |

| Water vapor meets cool air. | → | The cool air makes the water vapor Ⓑ _____. |

| Water drops get bigger and heavier. | → | Then they fall as Ⓒ _____ or Ⓓ _____. |

2. SUMMARIZE Write a sentence telling the main idea of this lesson.

3. VOCABULARY Use the word **condense** to tell about this picture.

Test Prep

4. Water moves from the land to the air and back again in the _____ .

A. water cycle
B. ocean
C. clouds
D. rain

Links

 Math

Use Ordinal Numbers
Work with a partner to draw the steps of the water cycle. Write about each step using **first**, **second**, **third**, and **fourth**.

 For more links and activities, go to www.hspscience.com

First, the sun heats the water.

295

What Are the Seasons?

Fast Fact

Early spring is the best time to plant a vegetable garden. You can hypothesize about what helps plants grow in spring.

296

Plants and Light

You need

 • **young plant**  • **shoe box with hole**   • **spray bottle**

Step 1

Spray the plant with water. Put it in the box. Put the lid on the box.

Step 2

Place the box so that the hole faces a window. **Hypothesize** about what will happen to the plant.

Step 3

Spray the plant with water each day. After one week, what happens? Was your **hypothesis** correct?

Inquiry Skill

When you **hypothesize**, you think of an idea.

297

Reading in Science

VOCABULARY
season
spring
summer
fall
winter

 READING FOCUS SKILL

MAIN IDEA AND DETAILS Look for the main ideas about spring.

Seasons

A **season** is a time of year. The seasons are spring, summer, fall, and winter.

Spring is the season after winter. In spring, the weather gets warmer. There may be many rainy days.

 MAIN IDEA AND DETAILS
What is the weather like in spring?

rain

How can you tell it is spring?

298

Plants and Animals in Spring

Many plants begin to grow in spring. They get more warmth, light, and rain than they got in winter.

In spring, many animals have their young. New plants are food for the young animals.

flowers

★ MAIN IDEA AND DETAILS
(Focus Skill) **Why do many plants grow well in spring?**

ewe and lambs

299

How can you tell it is summer?

Summer

Summer is the season after spring. Summer weather can be very hot. Some places may have thunderstorms.

Plants grow well in summer weather. Fruits start to grow on some plants.

tomato plant

⭐ **MAIN IDEA AND DETAILS**
What is summer?

300

Animals in Summer

Animals have ways to stay cool in summer. Some cool off in mud or water. Others lose fur so that their coats are lighter.

★ **MAIN IDEA AND DETAILS**

What is one way animals stay cool in summer?

pig cooling off in mud

bison shedding fur

301

Fall

Fall is the season after summer. In fall, the weather gets cooler.

In many places, leaves change color and fall from trees. Some fruits are ready to eat.

 MAIN IDEA AND DETAILS How does the weather change in fall?

trees in fall

squirrel carrying food

This hummingbird migrates in fall.

Animals in Fall

As the weather gets cooler, some animals migrate, or move to new places. There they can find more food and stay warm. Animals that do not migrate may grow a thicker coat or store food to eat later.

(Focus Skill) **MAIN IDEA AND DETAILS**
What do some animals do in fall?

Swim!

Why do people swim outdoors only in summer? Put a cup of water under a lamp. **CAUTION:** The lamp may be hot! Put another cup of water in a shady place. Which cup of water warms up faster?

Winter

Winter is the season after fall. In some places it gets very cold. Snow may fall.

Some plants rest in winter. They will start to grow again when it gets warmer in spring.

In winter, it is hard for animals to find food. Some eat food they stored earlier. Others sleep until spring.

cactuses in winter

MAIN IDEA AND DETAILS **How is winter different from fall?**

This bear will sleep until spring.

304

1. MAIN IDEA AND DETAILS Copy and complete this chart.

> **Seasons**

> **Main Idea**
> There are four seasons.

detail	detail	detail	detail
In **Ⓐ** _____, many animals have young.	In **Ⓑ** _____, many fruits grow.	In **Ⓒ** _____, some animals migrate.	In **Ⓓ** _____, it is hard for animals to find food.

2. DRAW CONCLUSIONS Why do you think some animals grow a thicker coat in fall?

3. VOCABULARY Tell about the **season** in this picture.

Test Prep

4. How can winter be different in different places?

Links

Math 1₂3

Use a Calendar

Use a calendar to answer these questions. How many months are there? What are their names? Which ones are summer months? When does summer begin? When does it end?

For more links and activities, go to www.hspscience.com

JUNE						
SUN	MON	TUE	WED	THU	FRI	SAT
			1	2	3	4
5	6	7	8	9	10	11
12	13	14	15	16	17	18
19	20	21	22	23	24	25
26	27	28	29	30		

Is the Weather Getting Worse?

Earth's weather can get pretty wild. Scientists say that Earth's weather is getting wilder. That's because Earth's temperature is rising.

Using Powerful Tools

Weather experts use satellites to study weather. Satellites with cameras are launched into space. The satellites take pictures showing Earth's weather.

306

The pictures are sent to weather experts. The experts then use computers. The computers help predict what the weather will be in the future.

Looking Back

Weather experts studied the weather of the past. They compared that weather with today's weather. The experts say the study shows that the world's weather is changing.

Scientists say the change is because Earth's temperature is rising. This change might mean less rain will fall in the future. Or, it may mean that summer weather will last longer.

Warming Warning!

Scientists say that the world's weather will keep getting worse if the warming does not stop.

THINK ABOUT IT

How do satellites help weather experts?

Spin In

Find out more! Log on to
www.hspscience.com

Watching the Weather

Bob Stokes is a special kind of scientist. He studies the weather. He can tell when the weather will change.

Stokes can also tell when a thunderstorm might happen. Thunderstorms can bring strong winds and heavy rain. They can harm people and their homes. If people know what kind of weather is coming, they can try to be safe. Stokes is helping people do that.

You Can Do It!

Explore Evaporation

What to Do

1. Put the same amount of water in each cup. Put a piece of tape on each cup to mark the waterline. Cover one cup tightly with plastic wrap.
2. Put both cups in a warm place.
3. Wait one day. Compare the water in the cups. Talk about what you see.

Materials

- 2 plastic cups
- water
- tape
- plastic wrap

Draw Conclusions

What happened to the water in each cup? Why do you think that happened?

Weather Safety

Make a poster about weather safety. Show ways you stay safe in different kinds of weather. Tell ways to stay safe in the sun, in snowstorms, and in rainstorms. Share your poster with the class.

Weather Safety
Wear sunscreen. Stay cool.
Wear warm clothes
Wear a raincoat. Go inside if the rain is heavy.

Review and Test Preparation

Vocabulary Review

Use these words to complete the sentences.

weather p. 284   **evaporate** p. 292

thermometer p. 287   **water vapor** p. 292

1. A tool that measures temperature is a ____.

2. Heat may cause water to ____.

3. Water in the air is ____.

4. What the air outside is like is ____.

Check Understanding

5. Look at the arrows that show the parts of the water cycle. What is the **cause** for each **effect?**

6. Which tool would you use to find out how fast the wind is blowing?

A. anemometer

C. thermometer

B. rain gauge

D. weather vane

7. What do some animals do in fall?

F. They lose fur.

G. They migrate.

H. They have young.

J. They sleep until spring.

Critical Thinking

8. You are getting dressed in spring. How can you make sure you wear the right clothes for the weather?

Weather Report

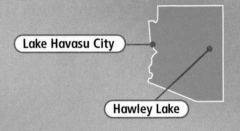

Lake Havasu City

Hawley Lake

What a hot place!

A Very Hot Place

Arizona is a hot state. The sun shines more strongly here than in some other states. This can make the temperature get very hot. Once it went up to 128°F! That was in Lake Havasu City.

C-O-L-D

Arizona can also get very cold. When the sun goes down, the temperature goes down, too. In Hawley Lake, it once went down to −40°F!

Brrr!

What makes it get so cold? Mountains, oceans, lakes, the wind, and storms can all change the temperature of the air.

Think and Do

1. SCIENCE AND TECHNOLOGY Why is knowing the temperature important? Some people need to know what the temperature is for their job. Choose one kind of work. Write sentences that tell why a person in this job needs to know the temperature.

2. SCIENTIFIC THINKING Think about the coldest temperature in Arizona. Now think about the hottest temperature. Draw a line down the middle of a sheet of paper. Write **hot** on one side and **cold** on the other. Then use pictures and words to tell what you would do for each kind of weather.

Sunset Crater

Sunset Crater
Volcano Park

Did you know there is a volcano in Arizona? Its name is Sunset Crater.

A long time ago, the volcano shot out lava, or rock that melted. The lava flowed over the land.

Over time, the lava cooled and got hard. It became a kind of rock.

Sunset Crater

Why Do Volcanoes Erupt?

The rock deep inside Earth is so hot that it melts. Sometimes the melted rock mixes with gases and rises up the cracks in a mountain. Then the mountain erupts, or blows its top!

Sunset Crater volcano got its name from the red and orange colors of its top. These are colors that you may see in a sunset.

A volcano blows its top!

Think and Do

1. SCIENTIFIC THINKING Look at a map of the United States. Are there other volcanoes near where you live? Choose one, draw it, and write about it.

2. SCIENTIFIC THINKING Scientists study volcanoes. They use machines that tell them if a volcano is going to erupt. Why is it important for scientists to study volcanoes? Use words and pictures to explain your ideas.

315

Canyon de Chelly National Monument

Canyon de Chelly National Monument

An Amazing Place

Native Americans have lived in Arizona for a long time. Some built homes in Canyon de Chelly, near Chinle.

The Anasazi, Pueblo, and Hopi people once lived here. Today, the Navajos live here.

The people who lived here long ago left things that tell us about them.

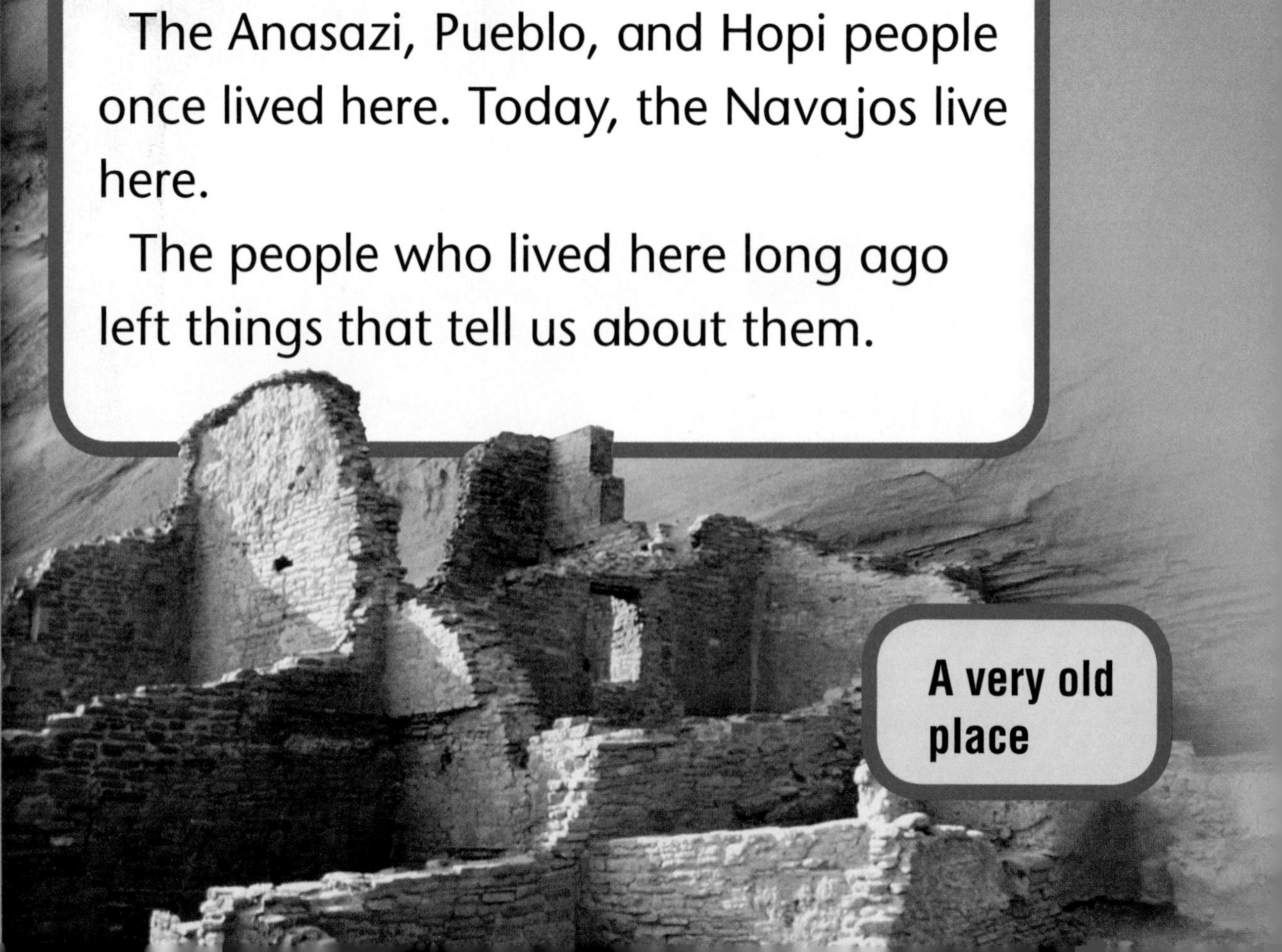

A very old place

316

People of Long Ago

The Native Americans who lived in Canyon de Chelly built their homes on cliffs. You can see these cliff homes at Canyon de Chelly National Monument.

The Native Americans used plants, such as the yucca, to make things. They made cords, sandals, and baskets.

The canyon walls are high.

Think and Do

1. **SCIENCE AND TECHNOLOGY** Native Americans built their homes on the sides of cliffs. How did they build in these high places? Use pictures and words to explain your ideas.

2. **SCIENTIFIC THINKING** National monuments protect places and things that are important. What special place would you choose to protect? Make a poster for your own "national monument." Draw and write to explain what makes that place special.

Are All Rocks the Same?

Materials
- rocks
- hand lens
- balance
- measuring tape

Procedure
1. Collect many different rocks.
2. Look at all the rocks.
3. Sort the rocks into groups.
4. Sort them in new ways.

Draw Conclusions
1. How are rocks alike and different?
2. What could you use a rock to make?

318

Trash Tally

Materials
• large box

Procedure
1. Place a large box next to your class trash can.
2. Put paper, plastic, and aluminum trash in the box. Put food and other messy trash in the trash can.
3. At the end of the day, look in the box.
4. At the end of the week, look in the box.

Draw Conclusions
1. What class trash could you reuse? Make a list.
2. What class trash could you recycle? Make a list.

References

Contents

Health Handbook

Reading in Science Handbook

Math in Science Handbook   R20

Your Senses

You have five senses that tell you about the world. Your five senses are sight, hearing, smell, taste, and touch.

Your Eyes

If you look at your eyes in a mirror, you will see an outer white part, a colored part called the iris, and a dark hole in the middle. This hole is called the pupil.

Caring for Your Eyes

- Have a doctor check your eyes to find out if they are healthy.

- Never look directly at the sun or at very bright lights.

- Wear sunglasses outdoors in bright sunlight and on snow and water.

- Don't touch or rub your eyes.

- Protect your eyes when you play sports.

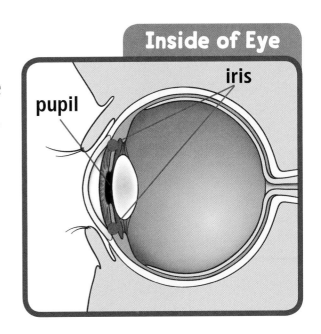

Inside of Eye

pupil iris

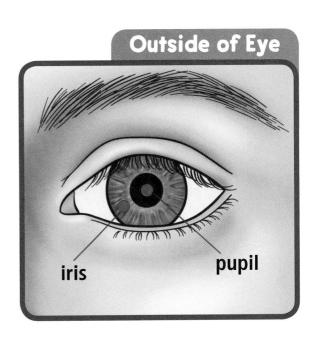

Outside of Eye

iris pupil

Your Senses

Your Ears

Your ears let you hear the things around you. You can see only a small part of the ear on the outside of your head. The parts of your ear inside your head are the parts that let you hear.

Caring for Your Ears

- Have a doctor check your ears.

- Avoid very loud noises.

- Never put anything in your ears.

- Protect your ears when you play sports.

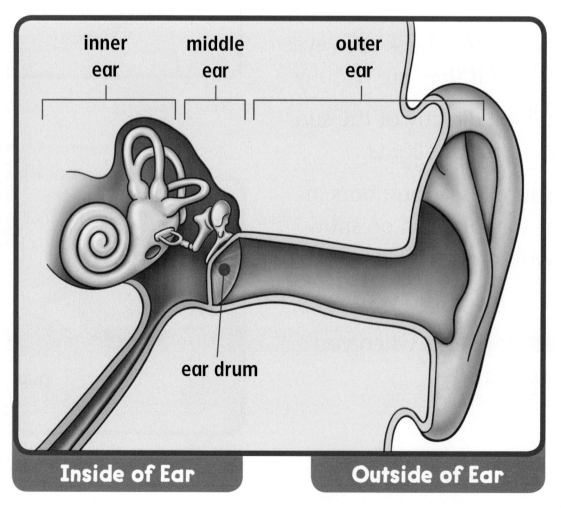

inner ear   middle ear   outer ear

ear drum

Inside of Ear   **Outside of Ear**

Your Senses of Smell and Taste

Your nose cleans the air you breathe and lets you smell things. Your nose and tongue help you taste things you eat and drink.

Your Skin

Your skin protects your body from germs. Your skin also gives you your sense of touch.

Caring for Your Skin

- Always wash your hands after coughing or blowing your nose, touching an animal, playing outside, or using the restroom.

- Protect your skin from sunburn. Wear a hat and clothes to cover your skin outdoors.

- Use sunscreen to protect your skin from the sun.

- Wear proper safety pads and a helmet when you play sports, ride a bike, or skate.

Your Skeletal System

Inside your body are many hard, strong bones. They form your skeletal system. The bones in your body protect parts inside your body.

Your skeletal system works with your muscular system to hold your body up and to give it shape.

Caring for Your Skeletal System

- Always wear a helmet and other safety gear when you skate, ride a bike or a scooter, or play sports.

- Eat foods that help keep your bones strong and hard.

- Exercise to help your bones stay strong and healthy.

- Get plenty of rest to help your bones grow.

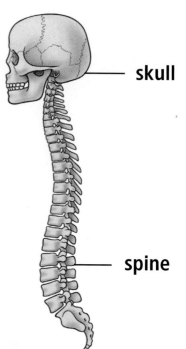

skull

spine

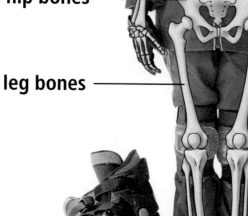

skull

arm bones

spine (backbone)

hip bones

leg bones

Your Muscular System

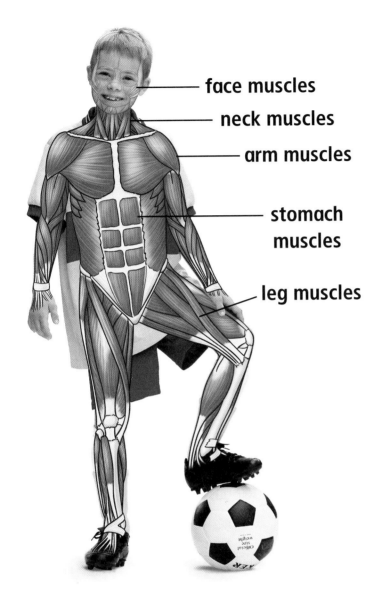

face muscles

neck muscles

arm muscles

stomach muscles

leg muscles

Your muscular system is made up of the muscles in your body. Muscles are body parts that help you move.

Caring for Your Muscular System

- Exercise to keep your muscles strong.

- Eat foods that will help your muscles grow.

- Drink plenty of water when you play sports or exercise.

- Rest your muscles after you exercise or play sports.

Your Nervous System

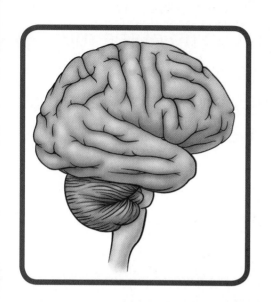

Your brain and your nerves are parts of your nervous system. Your brain keeps your body working. It tells you about the world around you. Your brain also lets you think, remember, and have feelings.

Caring for Your Nervous System

- Get plenty of sleep. Sleeping lets your brain rest.

- Always wear a helmet to protect your head and your brain when you ride a bike or play sports.

Your Digestive System

Your digestive system helps your body get energy from the foods you eat. Your body needs energy to do things.

When your body digests food, it breaks the food down. Your digestive system keeps the things your body needs. It also gets rid of the things your body does not need to keep.

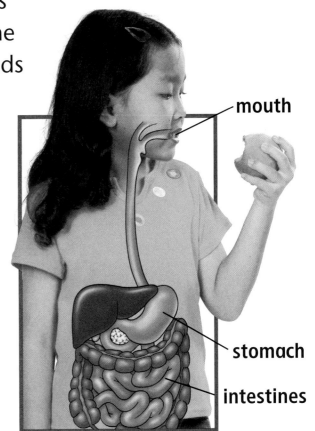

mouth

stomach

intestines

Caring for Your Digestive System

- Brush and floss your teeth every day.

- Wash your hands before you eat.

- Eat slowly and chew your food well before you swallow.

- Eat vegetables and fruits. They help move foods through your digestive system.

R7

Your Respiratory System

You breathe using your respiratory system. Your mouth, nose, and lungs are all parts of your respiratory system.

Caring for Your Respiratory System

• Never put anything in your nose.

• Never smoke.

• Exercise enough to make you breathe harder. Breathing harder makes your lungs stronger.

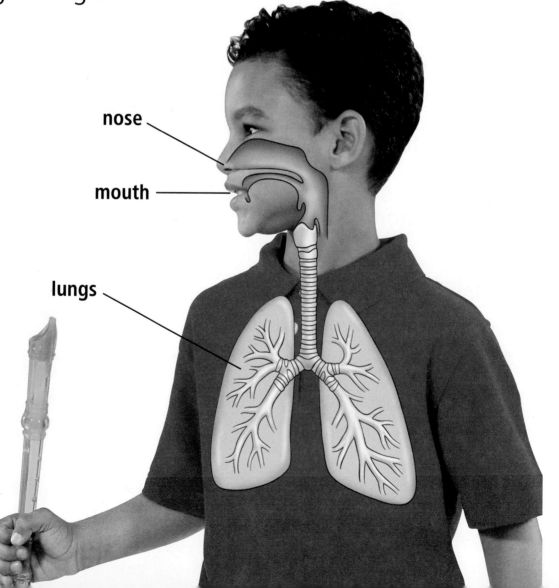

nose

mouth

lungs

Your Circulatory System

Your circulatory system is made up of your heart and your blood vessels. Your blood carries food energy and oxygen to help your body work. Blood vessels are small tubes. They carry blood from your heart to every part of your body.

Your heart is a muscle. It is beating all the time. As your heart beats, it pumps blood through your blood vessels.

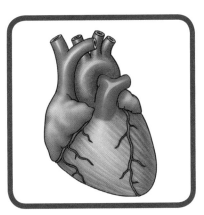

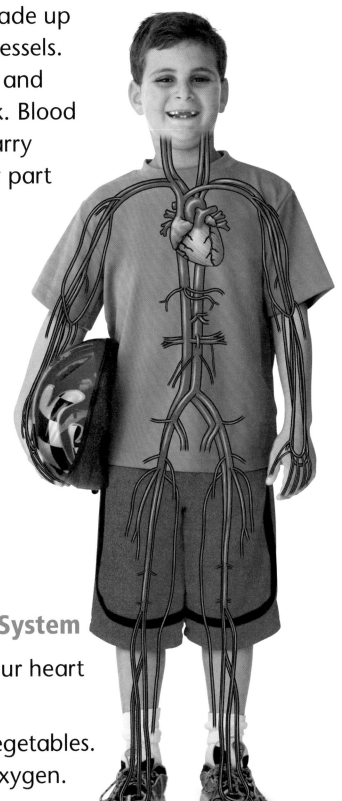

Caring for Your Circulatory System

• Exercise every day to keep your heart strong.

• Eat meats and green leafy vegetables. They help your blood carry oxygen.

• Never touch anyone else's blood.

Staying Healthy

You can do many things to help yourself stay fit and healthy.

You can also avoid doing things that can harm you.

If you know ways to stay safe and healthy and you do these things, you can help yourself have good health.

Getting enough rest

Staying away from alcohol, tobacco, and other drugs

Staying active

Keeping clean

Eating right

Keeping Clean

Keeping clean helps you stay healthy. You can pick up germs from the things you touch. Washing with soap and water helps remove germs from your skin.

Wash your hands for as long as it takes to say your ABCs. Always wash your hands at these times.

- Before and after you eat
- After coughing or blowing your nose
- After using the restroom
- After touching an animal
- After playing outside

Caring for Your Teeth

Brushing your teeth and gums keeps them clean and healthy. You should brush your teeth at least twice a day. Brush in the morning. Brush before you go to bed at night. It is also good to brush your teeth after you eat if you can.

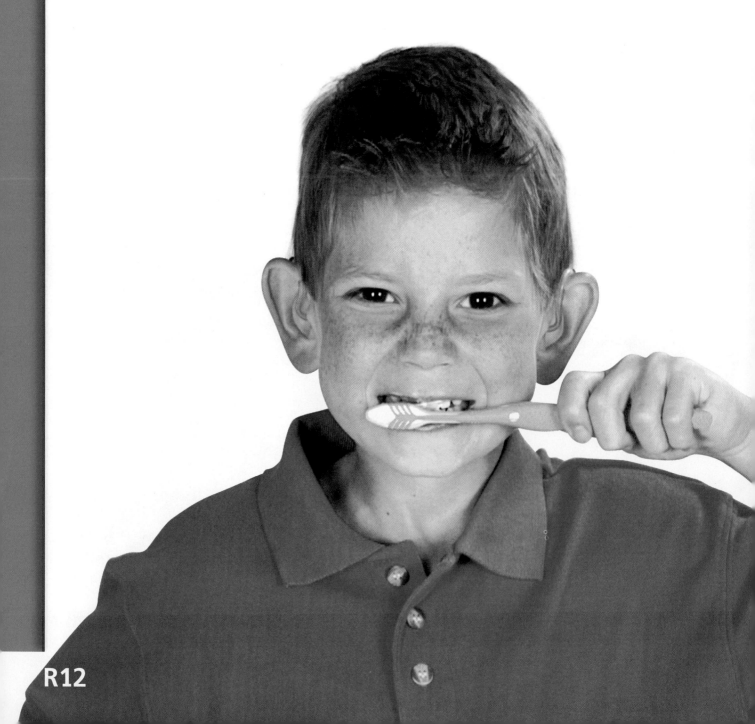

Brushing Your Teeth

Use a soft toothbrush that is the right size for you. Always use your own toothbrush. Use only a small amount of toothpaste. It should be about the size of a pea. Be sure to rinse your mouth with water after you brush your teeth.

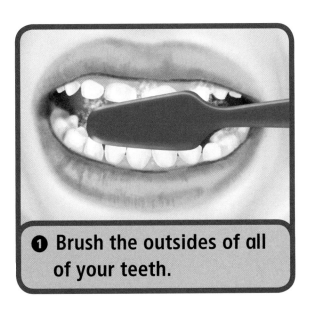

❶ Brush the outsides of all of your teeth.

❷ Brush the insides of all of your teeth.

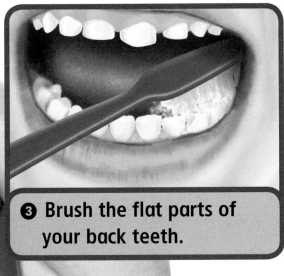

❸ Brush the flat parts of your back teeth.

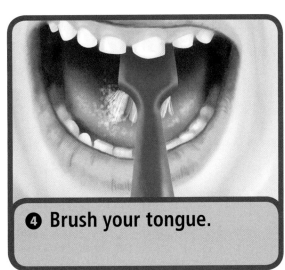

❹ Brush your tongue.

Identify the Main Idea and Details

Focus Skill

Some lessons in this science book are written to help you find the main idea. Learning how to find the main idea can help you understand what you read. The main idea of a paragraph is what it is mostly about. The details tell you more about it.

Read this paragraph.

> Lions are hunters. They hunt for meat to eat. Lions can run very fast. They see and hear very well. They need sharp teeth to catch animals. They have sharp teeth to eat the meat they catch.

This chart shows the main idea and details.

Detail: Lions can run very fast.	Detail: Lions see and hear very well.

Main Idea: Lions are hunters.

Detail: Lions hunt for meat to eat.	Detail: Lions have sharp teeth.

Compare and Contrast

Some science lessons are written to help you see how things are alike and different. Learning how to compare and contrast can help you understand what you read.

Read this paragraph.

> Birds and mammals are kinds of animals. Birds have a body covering of feathers. Mammals have a body covering of fur. Both birds and mammals need food, air, and water to live. Most birds can fly. Most mammals walk or run.

Here is how you can compare and contrast birds and mammals.

Ways They Are Alike	Ways They Are Different
Compare	**Contrast**
Both are kinds of animals. Both need food, air, and water to live.	Birds have feathers. Mammals have fur. Most birds fly. Most mammals walk or run.

Cause and Effect

Some science lessons are written to help you understand why things happen. You can use a chart like this to help you find cause and effect.

Cause	Effect
A cause is why something happens.	An effect is what happens.

Some paragraphs have more than one cause or effect. Read this paragraph.

> Water can be a solid, a liquid, or a gas. When water is very cold, it turns into solid ice. When water is heated, it turns into water vapor, a gas.

This chart shows the two causes and their effects in the paragraph.

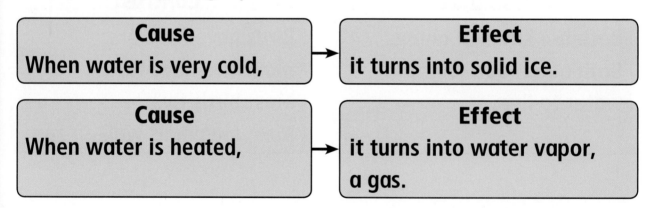

Cause	Effect
When water is very cold,	it turns into solid ice.

Cause	Effect
When water is heated,	it turns into water vapor, a gas.

Sequence

Focus Skill

Learning how to find sequence can help you understand what you read. You can use a chart like this to help you find sequence.

| 1. The first step. | → | 2. The next step. | → | 3. The last step. |

Some paragraphs use words that help you understand order. Read this paragraph. Look at the underlined words.

> Each day <u>begins</u> when the sun appears. <u>Then</u> the sun slowly climbs into the sky. At midday, the sun is straight overhead. <u>Then</u> the sun slowly falls back to the horizon. At <u>last</u>, the sun is gone. It is nighttime.

This chart shows the sequence of the paragraph.

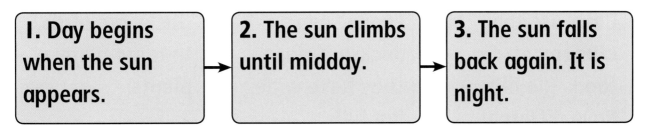

| 1. Day begins when the sun appears. | → | 2. The sun climbs until midday. | → | 3. The sun falls back again. It is night. |

Draw Conclusions

At the end of some lessons, you will be asked to draw conclusions. When you draw conclusions, you tell what you have learned. What you learned also includes your own ideas.

Read this paragraph.

> Birds use their bills to help them get food. Each kind of bird has its own kind of bill. Birds that eat seeds have strong, short bills. Birds that eat bugs have long, sharp bills. Birds that eat water plants have wide, flat bills.

This chart shows how you can draw conclusions.

What I Read		**What I Know**		**Conclusion:**
Birds use their bills to get food. The bills have different shapes.	+	I have seen ducks up close. They have wide, flat bills.	=	Ducks are birds that eat water plants.

Summarize

At the end of some lessons, you will be asked to summarize what you read. In a summary, some sentences tell the main idea. Some sentences tell details.

Read this paragraph.

> **Honey is made by bees. They gather nectar from flowers. Then they fly home to their beehive with the nectar inside special honey stomachs. The bees put the nectar into special honeycomb holes. Then the bees wait. Soon the nectar will change into sweet, sticky honey. The bees cover the holes with wax that they make. They eat some of the honey during the cold winter.**

This chart shows how to summarize what the paragraph is about.

Recall Detail	**Recall Detail**	**Recall Detail**
Honey is made by bees.	Bees gather nectar from flowers.	The nectar turns into honey in the beehive.

Summary

Bees make honey. They collect nectar from flowers. They bring the nectar to their beehive. The nectar turns to honey in the beehive.

Using Tables, Charts, and Graphs

Gathering Data

When you investigate in science, you need to collect data.

Suppose you want to find out what kinds of things are in soil. You can sort the things you find into groups.

Things I Found in One Cup of Soil

Parts of Plants

Small Rocks

Parts of Animals

By studying the circles, you can see the different items found in soil. However, you might display the data in a different way. For example, you could use a tally table.

Reading a Tally Table

You can show your data in a tally table.

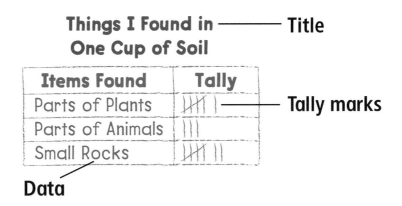

Things I Found in ——— Title
One Cup of Soil

Items Found	Tally
Parts of Plants	ⅠⅠⅠⅠ Ⅰ — Tally marks
Parts of Animals	ⅠⅠⅠ
Small Rocks	ⅠⅠⅠⅠ ⅠⅠ

Data

How to Read a Tally Table

1. **Read** the tally table. Use the labels.

2. **Study** the data.

3. **Count** the tally marks.

4. **Draw conclusions**. Ask yourself questions like the ones on this page.

Skills Practice

1. How many parts of plants were found in the soil?

2. How many more small rocks were found in the soil than parts of animals?

3. How many parts of plants and parts of animals were found?

Using Tables, Charts, and Graphs

Reading a Bar Graph

People keep many kinds of animals as pets. This bar graph shows the animal groups that pets belong to. A bar graph can be used to compare data.

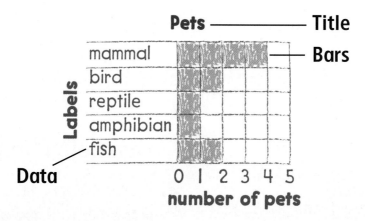

Title

Bars

Pets

mammal
bird
reptile
amphibian
fish

Labels

Data

0 1 2 3 4 5
number of pets

How to Read a Bar Graph

1. **Look** at the title to learn what kind of information is shown.

2. **Read** the graph. Use the labels.

3. **Study** the data. Compare the bars.

4. **Draw conclusions**. Ask yourself questions like the ones on this page.

Skills Practice

1. How many pets are mammals?

2. How many pets are birds?

3. How many more pets are mammals than fish?

Reading a Picture Graph

A second-grade class was asked to choose their favorite season. A picture graph was made to show the results. A picture graph uses pictures to show information.

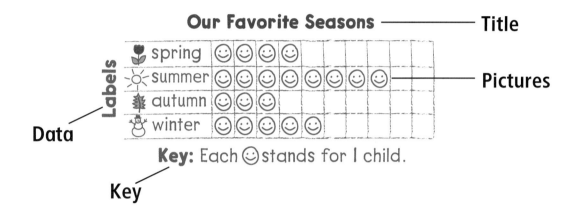

How to Read a Picture Graph

1. **Look** at the title to learn what kind of information is shown.

2. **Read** the graph. Use the labels.

3. **Study** the data. Compare the number of pictures in each row.

4. **Draw conclusions**. Ask yourself questions like the ones on this page.

Skills Practice

1. Which season did the most classmates choose?

2. Which season did the fewest classmates choose?

3. How many classmates in all chose summer or winter?

Measurements

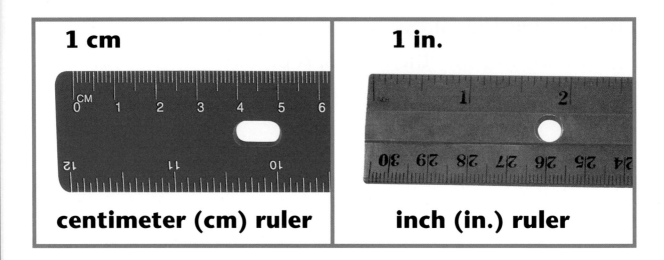

1 cm

centimeter (cm) ruler

1 in.

inch (in.) ruler

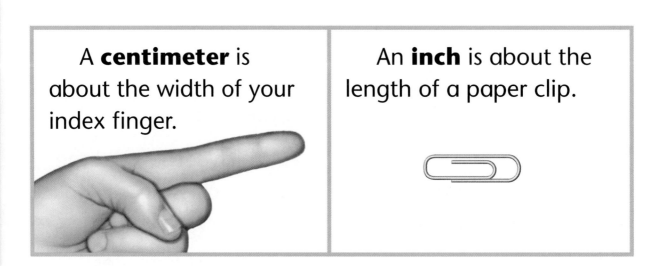

A **centimeter** is about the width of your index finger.

An **inch** is about the length of a paper clip.

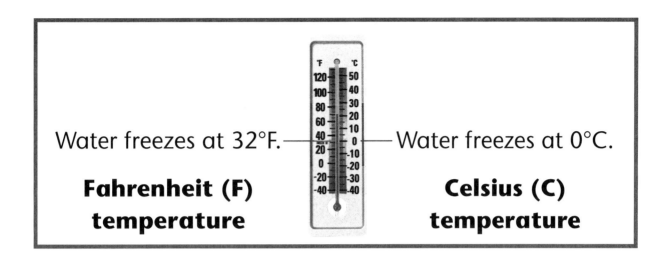

Water freezes at 32°F. ——————— Water freezes at 0°C.

Fahrenheit (F) temperature   **Celsius (C) temperature**

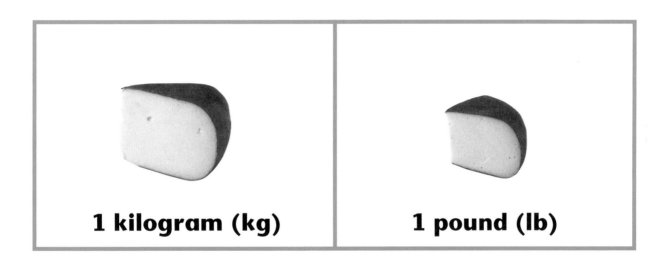

1 kilogram (kg)   **1 pound (lb)**

1 liter (L)   **1 cup (c)**

Safety in Science

Here are some safety rules to follow when you do activities.

1. **Think ahead.** Study the steps and follow them.

2. **Be neat and clean.** Wipe up spills right away.

3. **Watch your eyes.** Wear safety goggles when told to do so.

4. **Be careful with sharp things.**

5. **Do not eat or drink things.**

Visit the Multimedia Science Glossary to see illustrations of these words and to hear them pronounced.
www.hspscience.com

Glossary

A glossary lists words in alphabetical order. To find a word, look it up by its first letter or letters.

adaptation

A body part or behavior that helps a living thing. (112)

amphibian

A kind of animal that has smooth, wet skin. (46)

bird

The only kind of animal that has feathers. (45)

camouflage

A kind of adaptation in which an animal's color or pattern helps it hide. (116)

R27

condense

To change from water vapor into tiny water drops. The drops form clouds. (292)

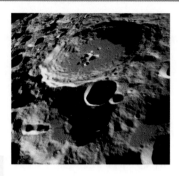

crater

A hole in a surface that is shaped like a bowl. The moon has many craters. (272)

desert

Land that gets very little rain. (142)

dissolve

To completely mix a solid with a liquid. (181)

edible

Safe to eat. (92)

environment

All the things that are in a place. (106)

E

evaporate

To change from liquid into water vapor. (292)

 F

fall

The season after summer. In fall, the air begins to get cooler. (302)

fish

A kind of animal that is covered in scales, uses gills to breathe, and lives in water. (47)

float

To stay on top of a liquid. (182)

flowers

The parts of a plant that make fruits. (78)

food chain

A diagram that shows how animals and plants are linked by what they eat. (124)

F

force

Something that makes an object move or stop moving. (202)

forest

Land that is covered with trees. (136)

fruits

The parts of a plant that hold the seeds. (78)

G

gills

The parts of a fish that take air from the water. (39)

H

habitat

The place where an animal finds food, water, and shelter. (138)

humus

Pieces of dead plants and animals. Humus, clay, and sand make up soil. (236)

inquiry skills

The skills people use to find out information. (12)

insect

A kind of animal that has three body parts and six legs. (48)

larva

Another name for a caterpillar. (54)

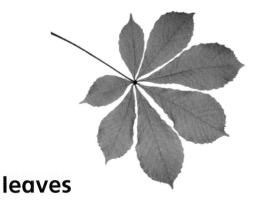

leaves

The parts of a plant that take in light and air to make food. (77)

length

The measure of how long a solid is. (176)

life cycle

All the parts of a plant's or animal's life. (52)

liquid

A kind of matter that flows and takes the shape of its container. (180)

living

Needing food, water, and air to grow and change. (32)

lungs

The parts of some animals that help them breathe air. Pigs are animals that use lungs to breathe. (39)

mammal

A kind of animal that has hair or fur and feeds its young milk. (44)

mass

The measure of how much matter something has. You can measure mass with a balance. (176)

matter

Everything around you. Matter can be a solid, liquid, or gas. (166)

M

mixture

Two or more things that have been mixed together. (174)

moon

A huge ball of rock in the sky that does not give off its own light. (259)

motion

A movement of something. Things are in motion when they move. (196)

N

natural resource

Anything from nature that people can use. (228)

nonedible

Not safe to eat. (93)

nonliving

Not needing food, water, and air and not growing. (33)

N

nutrients

Minerals in the soil that plants need to grow and stay healthy. (70)

O

oxygen

A kind of gas that plants give off and animals need to breathe. People need trees to get oxygen. (121)

P

pollen

A powder that flowers need to make seeds. Bees help carry pollen from one flower to another. (122)

pollution

Waste that causes harm to land, water, or air. (242)

pull

To tug an object closer to you. (203)

pupa

The part of a life cycle where a caterpillar changes into a butterfly. (54)

R34

P

push

To press an object away from you. (203)

R

recycle

To use old resources to make new things. (245)

reduce

To use less of a resource. (244)

reptile

A kind of animal that has scaly, dry skin. (46)

reuse

To use a resource again. (245)

rock

A hard, nonliving thing that comes from Earth. (234)

R

roots

The parts of a plant that hold it in the soil and take in water and nutrients. (75)

rotate

To spin around like a top. Earth rotates and causes day and night. (264)

S

science tools

The tools that help scientists find what they need. (20)

season

A season is a time of year. The seasons are spring, summer, fall, and winter. (298)

seed coat

A covering that protects a seed. (82)

seeds

The parts of a plant that new plants grow from. (78)

senses

The way we tell what the world is like. The five senses are sight, hearing, smell, taste, and touch. (4)

shelter

A place where animals can be safe. (40)

sink

To fall to the bottom of a liquid. (183)

soil

The top layer of Earth, made of sand, humus, and clay. (236)

solid

A kind of matter that keeps its shape. (173)

speed

The measure of how fast something moves. (197)

S

spring

The season after winter. In spring, the weather gets warmer. (298)

star

An object in the sky that gives off its own light. (258)

stem

The part of a plant that holds up the plant and lets food and water move through the plant. (76)

summer

The season after spring. It is usually hot. Summer has many hours of daylight. (300)

sun

The star closest to Earth. (258)

sunlight

Light that comes from the sun. (69)

tadpole

A young frog that comes out of an egg and has gills to breathe. (52)

temperature

The measure of how hot or cold something is. You can measure temperature with a thermometer. (287)

thermometer

A tool used to measure temperature. (287)

water cycle

The movement of water from Earth to the air and back again. (292)

water vapor

Water in the air that you can not see. (292)

weather

What the air outside is like. (284)

winter

The season after fall. It is usually cold. Winter has the fewest hours of daylight. (304)

Index

A

Adaptations
  of animal, 114–115
  of plant, 112–113
Air
  for animals, 39
  as natural resource, 228, 230
  as nonliving thing, 33
  for people, 230
  for plants, 68
  pollution, 242–243
Amphibians
  body coverings of, 46
  characteristics of, 46
  eggs of, 46
  frogs, 46, 52–53
Anemometer, 288
Animal Coverings, 27
Animals
  adaptations of, 114–115
  air for, 39, 230
  camouflage in, 116
  carrying pollen, 122
  carrying seeds, 123
  classify, 42–49
  in desert, 144
  in environments, 106–107
  in fall, 303
  in food chain, 124
  food for, 38
  in forest, 138

  growth of, 50–57
  habitat, 138
  helping plants, 113, 122–123
  and living and nonliving things, 30–35
  as living things, 32
  as natural resource, 228
  observe home of, 37
  oxygen for, 121
  pollution and, 242
  shelter for, 40, 120
  in spring, 299
  in summer, 301
  using plants, 120–121
  water for, 38
  in winter, 304
  See also Amphibians; Birds; Body coverings of animals; Fish; Insects; Mammals; Reptiles
Arizona Excursions Projects and Investigations, 152–159, 214–221, 312–319

B

Balance, 22
  to measure liquid, 184
  to measure mass, 176

Bar graph, R22
Bark
  compare leaves to, 135
  for protection, 113
Birds
  body coverings of, 45
  broad-tailed hummingbird, 303
  cactus wren, 156–157
  characteristics of, 45
  eagle, 138
  eggs of, 45
  feathers of, 45
  heron, 120
  hummingbird, 27, 113, 303
  owl, 40
  peacock, 45
  scarlet ibis, 114
  white-winged dove, 144
Bisbee, Arizona, 152–153
Body coverings of animals
  of amphibians, 46
  of birds, 45
  of fish, 47
  of insects, 48
  of mammals, 44
  of reptiles, 46
  in summer, 301
  Unit Experiment, 27
Body systems
  caring for teeth,

R

Photograph Credits

Page Placement Key: (t) top; (b) bottom; (c) center; (l) left; (r) right; (bg) background; (fg) foreground; (i) inset.

Cover
(front) Paul Nicklen/National Geographic/Getty Images; (back) Robert & Lorri Franz/Corbis; (back) (bg) Rosemary Calvert/Getty Images;

Front End Sheets
Page 1 (t) Alaska Stock Images; (bg) Alaska Stock Images; **Page 2** (t), (b) David W. Hamilton/Getty Images; (bg) Alaska Stock Images; **Page 3** (t) Alaska Stock Images; (b) Joel Sartore/National Geographic/Getty Images; (bg) Alaska Stock Images;

Title Page
Paul Nicklen/National Geographic/Getty Images;

Copyright Page
(inset) Paul Nicklen/National Geographic/Getty Images; (bg) Rosemary Calvert/Getty Images;

Back End Sheets
Page 1 (t) Thomas Mangelsen/Minden Pictures; (b) Norbert Rosing/National Geographic/Getty Images; (bg) Alaska Stock Images; **Page 2** (t) Yva Momatiuk/John Eastcott/Minden Pictures; (c) Paul Nicklen/National Geographic/Getty Images; (b) Alaska Stock Images; (bg) Alaska Stock Images; Page 3 (t) Klein/Hubert/Peter Arnold, Inc.; (b) Theo Allofs/Visuals Unlimited; (bg) Alaska Stock Images;

Table of Contents: iv Terry Donnelly/Alamy; vi Getty Images; vii Peter Arnold, Inc./Alamy.

Unit A
26 Terry Donnelly/Alamy; 27 (cr) Bruce Coleman Inc./Alamy; 28 Randy Wells/Corbis; 32 Getty Images; 34 (tl) Getty Images, (cl) A. & S. Carey/Masterfile, (bl) Paul Zahl/National Geographic Image Collection, (tr) Gary Thomas Sutto/Corbis, (cr) Getty Images, (br) Royalty-Free/Corbis; 35 Getty Images; 36 Michael & Patricia Fogden/Corbis; 38 (t) China Span/Animals Animals/Earth Scenes; (b) Winifred Wisniewski; Frank Lane Picture Agency/Corbis; 39 Kristian Cabanis/Age Fotostock; 40 (b) D. Robert & Lorri Franz/Corbis, (t) W. Perry Conway/Corbis; 41 D. Robert & Lorri Franz/Corbis; 42 Fritz Poelking/Age Fotostock; 44 (t) David Tipling/Nature Picture Library, (b) Tom Brakefield/Corbis; 45 (t) Robert Lubeck/Animals Animals/Earth Scenes, (b) John W. Bova/Photo Researchers; 46 (t) Darrell Gulin/Corbis, (c) Santiago Fernandez/Age Fotostock, (b) Marian Bacon/Animals Animals/Earth Scenes; 47 (t) Getty Images, (i) National Geographic/Getty Images, (b) Avi Klapfer/SeaPics.com; 48 (t) Paul Eekhoff/Masterfile, (c) IFA/eStock Photo/PictureQuest, (b) Jim Sugar/Corbis; 49 John W. Bova/Photo Researchers; 50 Norbert Rosing/National Geographic Image Collection; 54 E.R. Degginger/Color-Pic; 57 E.R. Degginger/Color-Pic, (b) Gary Meszaros/Photo Researchers; 58 (tl) Dr. Kenneth Lohmann/University of North Carolina; (b) Hamman Heldring of Animals Animals; 59 (tr) John Pontier/Animals Animals; (br) Dr. Kenneth Lohmann/University of North Carolina; 60 Annie Griffiths/Corbis; 61 (bg) PictureQuest; 62 (tl) Robert Lubeck/Animals Animals/Earth Scenes, (tlc) Paul Eekhoff/Masterfile, (trc) Tom Brakefield/Corbis; (tr) Avi Klapfer/SeaPics.com; (b) E.R. Degginger/Color-Pic; 63 John Staples; Cordaly Photo Library Ltd./Corbis; 64 Royalty-free/Corbis; 66 Carolynn Shelby/Alamy Images; 68 Freeman Patterson/Masterfile; 69 Tom Stewart/Corbis; 75 (l) Visuals Unlimited, (r) Paul Souders/IPNSTOCK.com, (bg) Alamy Images; 76 Gordon R. Gainer/Corbis; 77 (tl) Royalty-free/Corbis, (tr) Charles Mauzy/Corbis, (bl) Rob and Ann Simpson/Visuals Unlimited, (br) Barry Runk/Grant Heilman Photography; 78 (t) Bill Ross/Corbis, (b) Digital Vision (Royalty-free)/Getty Images; 80 Getty Images; 82 (c) Jerome Wexler/Photo Researchers, 83 (l) Michael P. Gadomski/Photo Researchers, (r) Jeff Lepore/Photo Researchers; 84 (c) David Sieren/Visuals Unlimited 85 (t) Ned Therrien/Visuals Unlimited; 86 (tr) Getty Images, (c) D. Cavagnaro/DRK, (tl) Mary Ellen Bartley/PictureArts/Corbis; 87 Ned Therrien/Visuals Unlimited; (b) Jerome Wexler/Photo Researchers; 88 Digital Vision (Royalty-free)/Getty Images; 90 (bg) Panoramic Images; (t) Valerie Giles/Photo Researchers; 91 (t) Michael Gadomski/Animals Animals/Earth Scenes; (b) George Harrison/Grant Heilman Photography; 92 Getty Images; 93 Liz Barry/Lonely Planet Images; 95 Bill Ross/Corbis; 96-97 Michigan State University Archives; 98 (both) AP/Wide World Photos; 99 (bg) Getty Images, Roger Wilmshurst; Frank Lane Picture Agency/Corbis; 101 Ken Wardius/Index Stock Imagery;

102 National Geographic/Getty Images; 104 William Ervin/Photo Researchers; 106 Patti Murray/Animals Animals/Earth Scenes; 108 Getty Images; 109 Patti Murray/Animals Animals/Earth Scenes; 110 Kevin Leigh/Index Stock Imagery; 112 (b) Alamy Images, (t) Alamy Images; 113 (t) Niall Benvie/Corbis, (bl) Francois Gohier/Photo Researchers; 114 (bg) T. Allofs/Zefa, (t) Roland Seitre/Peter Arnold, Inc., (c) Norman Owen Tomalin/Bruce Coleman, Inc.; 115 (l) Alamy Images, (r) ABPL Image Library/Animals Animals/Earth Scenes; 116 (tl) Yva Momatiuk/John Eastcott/Minden Pictures, (tr) Tom Walker/Visuals Unlimited, (bl) Seapics.com, (bc) Ken Thomas/Photo Researchers, (br) Bernard Photo Productions/Animals Animals/Earth Scenes; 118 John Vucci/Peter Arnold, Inc.; 120 (t) Galen Rowell/Corbis, (bl) Alamy Images, (br) Bruce Coleman, Inc.; 121 McDonald Wildlife Photography/Animals Animals/Earth Scenes; 122 (l) Jonathan Blair/National Geographic Image Collection; (b) Wild & Natural/Animals Animals/Earth Scenes; 123 (t) Eric and David Hosking/Corbis; (b) John Pontier/Animals Animals/Earth Scenes; 125 John Vucci/Peter Arnold, Inc.; 126 Harcourt Index; 127 AFP/Getty; 128 (c) Scott Camazine/Photo Researchers; (b) Stephen Dunn/The Hartford Courant; 129 (bg) Creatas Royalty Free Stock Resources; 132 Brand X Pictures/PictureQuest; 134 Alamy Images; 136 Grant Heilman/Grant Heilman Photography; 137 (t) Sharon Cummings/Dembinsky Photo Associates, (b) Hal Horwitz/Corbis, 138 (t) Photodisc Green (Royalty-free)/Corbis, (i) D. Robert Franz/Bruce Coleman, Inc., (b) Getty Images; 139 Getty Images; 140 Sally A. Morgan; Ecoscene/Corbis; 142 (bg) Andrew Brown; Ecoscene/Corbis, (t) Donald F. Thomas/Bruce Coleman, Inc.; 143 Getty Images; 144 (t) Joe McDonald/Corbis; (lc) Craig K. Lorenz/Photo Researchers, (b) Ted Levin/Animals Animals/Earth Scenes; 145 Andrew Brown; Ecoscene/Corbis; 146 (c) AP/Wide World Photos, (c) NASA; 147 (t) AP/Wide World Photos; 148 (bg) Ron Watts/Corbis; (t) Photodisc/Getty; 149 (bg) Dana Hursey/Masterfile; 150 (l) Craig K. Lorenz/Photo Researchers; (r) Getty Images; 152 (cr) Peter Arnold, Inc./Alamy; (b) Theo Allofs/Corbis; 153 (t) Rick and Nora Bowers/Visuals Unlimited; 154 (both) Grand Canyon Deer Farm; 155 Niebrugge Images; 156 Rick and Nora Bowers/Visuals Unlimited; 157 National Geographic/Getty Images.

Unit B
160 Albuquerque International Balloon Fiesta; 161 Philip Gould/CORBIS; 162 Photodisc Green/Getty; 170 Alamy Images; (bg) Dave G. Houser/Corbis; 172 Jose Luis Pelaez, Inc./Corbis; 173 (t) Jose Luis Pelaez, Inc./Corbis; 186 (t) Andy Levin/Photo Researchers; 187 (t) Craig Aurness/Corbis; 188 Lester Lefkowitz/Corbis; 189 (bg) Digital Vision(Royalty-free)/Getty Images; 192 Bill Bachmann/Photo Edit; 194 Bob Gelberg/Masterfile; 194 (bg) Ron Watts/Corbis, (i) Photodisc/Getty; 197 (t) Peter Walton/Index Stock Imagery; (b) Myrleen Ferguson Cate/Photo Edit; 198 (t) Bill Stevensen/SuperStock, (cl) Spencer Grant/Photo Edit, (cr) Mark E. Gibson/Corbis, (b) Wally McNamee/Corbis; 199 Bill Stevensen/SuperStock; 200 David Woods/Corbis; 204 (bg) Alamy Images; (b) Table Mesa Prod/Index Stock Imagery; 205 Myrleen Ferguson Cate/Photo Edit; 207 Myrleen Ferguson Cate/Photo Edit; 209 Photodisc/Getty; 210 Little blue Wolf, Productions/Corbis; 214 Roger Bickel/Mira.com; 215 (cl) David H. Smith; (cr) Getty Images; 216 Deer Valley Rock Art Center; 217 John Oeth/Alamy; 218 (inset) Philip Coblentz Picture Arts Corp./Robertstock.com; 218-219 (spread) Steve Thornton/Corbis

Unit C
222 David Parker/Science Photo Library/Photo Researchers, Inc.; 224 Garry Black/Masterfile; 226 Johnathan Smith; Cordaly Photo Library Ltd./Corbis; 228 Getty Images; 229 (l) Jose Luis Pelaez/Corbis; 230 (t) Getty Images, (l) Workbookstock.com; 231 Getty Images; 232 Getty Images; 234 (t) Gerald and Buff Corsi/Visuals Unlimited, (b) Lee Snider/Photo Images/Corbis; 235 (t) Getty Images, (ti) Breck P. Kent Photography, (b) Photodisc Green(Royalty-free)/Getty Images, (bi) Massimo Listri/Corbis; 237 (t) David Young-Wolff/PhotoEdit, (b) Paul A. Souders/Corbis; 239 Charles O'Rear/Corbis; 240 Play Mart, Inc.; 243 (t) Stockbyte/PictureQuest, (b) Kathy McLaughlin/The Image Works; 245 David Young-Wolff/PhotoEdit; 247 Alamy Images; 248 Brian Sytnyk/Masterfile; 249 Don Smetzer/Photo Edit; 250 (t) Ewell Sale Stewart Library/The Academy of Natural Sciences; (b) Martin Garwood/Photo Researchers; 251 (bg) National Geographic/Getty Images; 252 (t) Myrleen Cate/Index Stock Imagery, (cb) Photodisc Green (Royalty-free)/Getty Images (b) Getty Images; 253 (t) Angela Hampton; Ecoscene/Corbis; 254 Astrofoto/Peter Arnold, Inc.; 256 Creative Concept/Index Stock Imagery; 258 Getty Images; 259 (t) Roger Ressmeyer/Corbis; 260 (cr) Stocktrek/Corbis; 261 G. Kalt/Masterfile; 262 Corbis; 264 (b) Getty Images; 265 (b) Zefa Visual Media - Germany/Index Stock Imagery; 268 Corbis; 270 (bg) Rev. Ronald Royer/Science Photo Library/Photo Researchers; (cr) Larry Landolfi/Photo Researchers; 271 (t, r) Larry Landolfi/Photo Researchers; (b) Eckhard Slawik/Photo Researchers; 272 (bg) NASA/Photo Researchers, (l) Bettmann/Corbis, (r) NASA/Photo Researchers; 273 (c) 1966 Corbis; Original image courtesy of NASA/Corbis; 274-275 (all) NASA; 277 (bg) Gabe Palmer/Corbis; 276 (t) NASA, (c) Wide World Photos; (c, b) NASA/JPC/Cornell; 279 (tr) Eckhard Slawik/Photo Researchers; (tl, cl, cr) Larry Landolfi/Photo Researchers; (b) Alamy Images; 280 Michael Deyoung/Age Fotostock; 282 Getty Images; 284 (bg) Leng/Leng/Corbis; (t) Mark Polott/Index Stock Imagery; (b) William Manning/Corbis; 285 (t) Craig Tutttle/Corbis; 286 (bg) Digital Vision; (b) Royalty-free/Corbis; 287 (b) Workbookstock.com; 288 (t) Jeff Greenberg/Index Stock Imagery; (c) Tony Freeman/PhotoEdit; 290 Jim Reed/Corbis; 294 (t) Royalty-free/Corbis; (c) Jonathan Nourok/PhotoEdit; (b) Royalty-free/Corbis; 295 Royalty-free Corbis; 296 George H. H. Huey/Corbis; 298 (t) Richard Hutchings/PhotoEdit; 299 (t) Eric Cricton/Corbis; (b) Royalty-Free/CORBIS; 300 (t) Bill Bachmann/Alamy; (b) Christi Carter/Grand Heilman Photography; 301 (t) Digital Vision/Getty Images; (b) Phil Schermeister/CORBIS; 302 MedioImages; 303 (l) Florian Moellers/Age Fotostock; (r) Ray Coleman/Science Photo Library/Photo Researchers, Inc.; 304 (t) Peter Arnold, Inc./Alamy; (b) William Ervin/Photo Researchers; 305 Christi Carter/Grand Heilman Photography; 306 (tl) AP/Wide World Photos; (br) NASA; 308 Courtesy the Weather Channel; 311 (tl) Tony Freeman/PhotoEdit; (br) Jeff Greenberg/Index Stock Imagery; 312 (b) Jason Edwards/National Geographic Society Image Collection; (cr) BananaStock/Alamy; 313 Brand X Pictures/Alamy; 314 Tom Bean; 315 Getty Images; 316 Jack Parsons/Omni-Photo; 317 Getty Images.

Glossary
R27 (cl) APBPL Image Library/Animals Animals/Earth Scenes; (cr) Marian Bacon/Animals Animals/Earth Scenes; (bl) John W. Bova/Photo Researchers; (br) Yva Momatiuk/John Eastcott/Minden Pictures; R28 (tl) Royalty-free Corbis; (tr) © 1966 Corbis/Original image courtesy of NASA/Corbis; (cl) Andrew Brown; Ecoscene/Corbis; (br) Patti Murray/Animals Animals/Earth Scenes; (cl) Avi Klapfer/SeaPics.com; (bl) Michael P. Gadomski/Photo Researchers; R30 (tl) Alamy Images; (tr) Grant Heilman/Grant Heilman Photography; Bill Ross/Corbis; (cr) Kristian Cabanis/Age Fotostock; (bl) Craig K. Lorenz/**Photo Researchers; R31 Paul Eekhoff/Masterfile; (cl) E.R. Degginger/Color-Pic; Barry Runk/Grant Heilman Photography; R32 (tr) Paul Zahl/National Geographic Image Collection; R33 (tr)** Rev. Ronald Royer/Science Photo Library/Photo Researchers; (cl) Bob Gelberg/Masterfile; (bl) Liz Barry/Lonely Planet Images; (br) Gary Thomas Sutto/Corbis; R34 (cl) John Vucci/Peter Arnold; (br) E.R. Degginger/Color-Pic; R35 (cr) Santiago Fernandez/Age Fotostock; R36 (tl) Visuals Unlimited; (cr) Matheisi/Taxi/Getty Images; (bl) Jerome Wexler/Photo Researchers; (br) Digital Sieren/Visuals Unlimited; R37 (tr) W. Perry Conway/Crobis; (bl) Jose Luis Pelaez, Inc./Corbis; (br) Peter Walton/Index Stock Imagery; R38 (tl) John Colwell/Grant Heilman Photography; (tr) Creative Concept/Index Stock Imagery; (cr) Alamy Images; (bl) Getty Images; (br) Freeman Patterson/Masterfile; R39 Getty Images; (br) Royalty-free Corbis; (t) Robert Frerck/Odyssey/Chicago.

SELF-PROTECTION An arctic fox curls up in the snow. Then it covers its nose and face with its tail.

YOUNG An arctic fox gives birth to 4-11 pups at a time.

BEHAVIOR The arctic fox stores food during the summer.

CAMOUFLAGE The arctic fox has fur that changes color with the season.

SELF-PROTECTION Thick fur keeps an arctic fox's feet warm.